ADI SHANKARACHARYA'S
BHAJA GOVINDAM

ADI SHANKARACHARYA'S
BHAJA GOVINDAM
SEEKING AND FINDING ANSWERS WITHIN

SWAMI
SUKHABODHANANDA

JAICO PUBLISHING HOUSE

Ahmedabad Bangalore Bhopal Chennai
Delhi Hyderabad Kolkata Lucknow Mumbai

Published by Jaico Publishing House
A-2 Jash Chambers, 7-A Sir Phirozshah Mehta Road
Fort, Mumbai - 400 001
jaicopub@jaicobooks.com
www.jaicobooks.com

Published in arrangement with
Prasanna Trust
No. 51, 16th Cross, Between 6th & 8th Main
Malleswaram, Bangalore 560 055, India

ADI SHANKARACHARYA'S BHAJA GOVINDAM
ISBN 978-81-8495-206-3

First Jaico Impression: 2011
Second Jaico Impression: 2011

Printed by
Rashmi Graphics
#3, Amrutwel CHS Ltd., C.S. #50/74
Ganesh Galli, Lalbaug, Mumbai-400 012
E-mail: tiwarijp@vsnl.net

About the Author

Swami Sukhabodhananda is the founder Chairman of Prasanna Trust. Swamiji is not only one of the most respected spiritual leaders of the country, but is also nicknamed as 'Corporate Guru'. His expertise lies in synthesizing ancient wisdom of east and modern vision of west appealing to both the young and old from a wide spectrum of society.

Swamiji is the author of many best sellers whose books have sold over a million in more than 79 titles in different languages. His books have made many discover a new way of living life. He makes you realise that if one door closes another door opens. Life is an opening.

His self-development programs have benefited many in the corporate sectors of reputed institutions like banking, finance, industry, education, armed forces and police.

Leading industrial houses invite him to conduct 'In-house workshops' for their executives.

Swamji is also a Sport Psychology coach for cricket teams like Delhi Dare Devils and many others.

'Times of India' in their recent poll on 'who talks the best' places Swamiji as the one, who tops the list on all counts as the best speaker.

'The Week' magazine acclaims Swamiji as one among the top five best exponent of spiritual knowledge.

Swamiji's English books *'Oh, Mind Relax Please!'* and *'Oh, Life Relax Please!'* are the top best sellers in the country and has set a new bench mark in the lives of many, from the Kargil hero Gen. V. P. Malik who swear by the inspiring content of the book to the New York Mayor who acknowledges its usefulness to diminish work pressure and dealing with New York City press!

Swamiji's book *'Manase Relax Please'* has set an all time sales record in the history of Tamil, Kannada and Telugu books and has been included as a part of curriculum in some of the schools and colleges. Leading personalities have termed that he has revolutionised Tamil literature through his books.

Swamiji was invited as a dignitary on five different panels at the World Economic Forum in Davos, Switzerland and was a special invitee to the United Nation World Millennium Summit of spiritual Leaders.

Swamiji is the second Indian to be honored at the prestigious lotus millionaires' Intellectual Club at Manhattan, New York.

Swamiji's works in audio and video have been transforming the lives of many through Sa Re Ga Ma and Times Music.

His message on the Aastha, Sanskar and many other Channels is reaching a wide spectrum of people both in India and Overseas.

Prasanna Trust under his inspiration and guidance runs an orphanage for girls, provides artificial limbs and calipers to people with impoverished background and conducts regular blood donation camps and camps for feeding the poor.

Swamiji was awarded 'Karnataka's Best Social Service Award' by Essel group & Zee network.

Preface

To be sensitive to follow the footsteps of the wise and to seek what they have sought and not be caught in their footsteps is the contradiction of the spiritual path. The great revolutionary saint through these simple poetic verses unfolds the secrets of wise living.

The sensitive search has to be found in everyday life but alas, one gets stuck to mundane everydayness of life and thus misses the magic of living life wisely. To be aware of the possibility of the search is a gift we owe ourselves. To miss this is to be in despair in a spiritual sense.

It is one thing to be clear of the end of the journey but it is the wise journey which truly matters in the end. I have put in my love and experience in commenting on these famed, most revered verses. The commentaries of these verses are not meant to be taught but it is more of expressing my journey which is unfolding to the music of the spiritual path.

The purpose of the 'fish net' is to catch fishes; once it is caught the net is not important. The purpose of these words is to convey the mystery of the spiritual path and its goal; once this is grasped the words become redundant.

The world is ever charged with divinity. But when one is filled with mundane activities, one misses the divine flavor. Never make this mistake. Flow with life, grow with life, and renounce the unessential. Let the unessential remind you of the essential and thus be alive with the essential.

If one has eyes to see, one will see that this very world is soaked in heaven. Even a blade of grass is a flame or an expression of godliness. Seeing this, one will take off one's psychological shoes of vanity and touch the world with wordless reverence.

The poetic words of the master are revolutionary and it is relevant even in today's world that is divided, in conflict, repressed and unbalanced. The unhappiness is spread all around in spite of material abundance. The real answers to the core weakness of humanity are hidden in these verses.

I pray and hope you benefit from these verses and my commentaries on them. I thank P.R. Madhav for lovingly editing this book. I deeply thank Mrs Deviki Jaipuria and my loving mother as a source of inspiration and support for all my endeavours. I thank all my students who have helped me to make a difference to the world.

Let us join the company of the wise and know the delight of the soul. Let us transform one's burning heart into a healing heart and live the language of the wise.

—Swami Sukhabodhananda

Contents

Contents

Our heartfelt thanks to all enlightened masters and
modern thinkers for their inspirational guidance.

Adi Shankaracharya's

Bhaja Govindam
Seeking and Finding Answers Within

We will be starting a new series of talks on one of the great works of Adi Shankaracharya known as *Bhaja Govindam*.

'*Bhaja*' literally means 'seek', '*Govindam*' means 'the Lord' — 'the Truth'.

A rich man wanted to experiment. He chose one of the most beautiful islands as a retreat. He stayed there for years. One day he thought he had lived enough with nature and decided to come back to his hometown... New York City. He had lived for nearly thirty years in that beautiful Island. Upon his return, some of the journalists were curious to interview him and wanted him to share about his beautiful holiday lasting over thirty years.

They began asking many questions about the island as it was supposed to be unbelievably beautiful. People were asking questions such as, 'How the island was? What was his experience? What were the seasonal changes about the flora and fauna? Did he encounter any wildlife experience?

1

What made him stay so long in one island?'... He heard all their queries patiently and at the end said, 'My God, I did not know the island was so beautiful. If only I had known about its beauty earlier, I would have looked at each element more closely'.

When I read this example, I found similarity in our lives too. Here was a man who lived in a beautiful island, and because the journalists were interviewing him, he said, 'If only I had known about its beauty earlier, I would have looked at each element more closely'.

In life we do not observe things closely. And when we don't observe things closely, we start looking at things very superficially. Living life superficially means living a life of deficiency — *samsaara*, and living life deeply is living a life of inner freedom — *nirvana*.

Please look at it this way; living a life of deficiency — *samsaara*, is similar to looking at life superficially. It is like a rich man from the above example staying in the island and superficially viewing the island over 30 years. But if he had lived life deeply and totally, he would have been able to see and experience the beauty and the grandeur of the island as the great Saint Adi Shankaracharya says, '*Soundarya Lahari*', — *Lahari* means waves, *Soundarya* means beauty. Adi Shankaracharya has written a book on *Soundarya Lahari* — where he details that everything is a wave and waves and waves of beauty.

All enlightened masters, out of deep compassion try to wake up humanity. They try to wake up humanity because humanity has been living in their basement of life. To drive home the point, just imagine a multistorey building. Suppose, you are living in the basement and you have not explored the other floors of the building. If you are only looking at the basement of the multi-storey building, your view of the world from the basement is going to be limited. If a consultant comes and says — you are living in a multi-storey building, why are you just living at the basement? How ridiculous and foolish it looks.

If you are the owner of the multi-storey building, why don't you explore all the way.

I am saying this because throughout the verses of *Bhaja Govindam,* Adi Shankaracharya says, 'Oh, Fool! *Mudhamate, mudhamate, mudhamate.* He says this out of deep love as we are living a lukewarm life. We are not living a life of real in totality and therefore please see, throughout the whole unfoldment of *Bhaja Govindam,* he is inviting us to wake up to a higher dimension of living. When we open our eyes; our third eye, we see *Soundarya lahari* — waves and waves of beauty.

The narration of *Bhaja Govindam* emerged when Adi Shankaracharya was on a journey by foot along with his disciples. As he was walking, he found a very old man rattling out the ancient Sanskrit grammar-rules — *vyakarana.* This old man who was in his twilight of life span was still learning grammar-rules — *vyakarana.* Grammar rule is a very difficult subject to learn. Some of you may say *vyakarna ko padke kya karna.* Grammar is a very beautiful subject no doubt, but learning such texts at a ripe old age is leading life in an improper perspective. This old man was still learning grammar rules — I VUN

3

VUL RUK YE VONG I VOUCH HAYAVARAT LAN
JABAGHAN GADADHASH JABAGADADHASH
CHAPAKATATAU KAPAI SA SHA SAR HAL iti
maheswara sutrani.

The basic grammar rule from where you begin with is, *I
vun vul ruk* and so on. It is from there the grammar
emerges. Whereas this old gentlemen was still at learning
basic grammar rules. Adi Shankaracharya took pity on him
and said, 'At this ripe old age learning basic grammar-rules
is not worthwhile, please get up and don't be foolish.
Don't live this type of a life. *Mudhamate,* Oh, Fool!' And
thus he unfolds the verses of *Bhaja Govindam.*

Subsequently, the disciples of Adi Shankaracharya started
adding more verses. For example, Sureshacharya,
Totakacharya, Hastamalaka went on adding more verses at
the end portion of the *Bhaja Govindam.* The whole text of
Bhaja Govindam in essence means 'Wake up, Seek the Lord,
and stop seeking for primitive things in life. Stop seeking
the superficial things in life. Stop seeking the unessential
things in life.' Therefore the whole text of *Bhaja Govindam*
has to be listened from a sincere heart. I always say, 'The
heart of education is the education of the heart.'

When we don't listen to it from our heart, we find when
Adi Shankaracharya terms one as a fool, it appears as if his
statement is very cruel, and arrogant. But it is not so. It is
out of deep love, this great enlightened master disturbs
our slumber of being in living a life of deficiency —
Samsaara. Please get this rightly – all great enlightened
masters' teachings appear disturbing our slumber, and
initially it is upsetting. Jesus Christ was crucified, Socrates

was poisoned, Mansoor was killed. Adi Shankaracharya was called as a disguised Buddhist — *Prachanna Bhoudha*. Scholars started calling him names.

These enlightened masters disturb our slumber but they don't put us to sleep. We are cozily asleep, lost in our belief and in our dogmas; they come and wake us up, shake us up and pull us out from our comfort zone, which is *not* really our comfort zone. It is only supporting our lethargy. Our comfort zone is not really allowing us to grow. It is protecting us and cementing our lethargy. Therefore, great saints' call is to wake us up. All words of enlightened masters are really an invitation to waking us up.

Thus, one has to listen to the words of Adi Shankaracharya from such perceptive. I have always been emphasizing that when you listen, listen very carefully. More often people listen from different dimensions.

Some students' listening are something like what I call as a dosa pan. A dosa pan is a pan on which you make dosas. The pan is heated and when water is sprinkled, it immediately evaporates. Some students are like a dosa pan – very hot with their tensions, hot with their arrogance, hot with their conclusions, hot with their dogmas; and when the master's cool words fall on their ears they just get burnt away. It gets evaporated. So long as one listens to the master's words, some coolness may be present but the moment the teaching stops, it disappears in them however the speech — *vaani*, may be cool — *sheetal*. Kabir in one of his couplets *(doha)*, says,

Aisi vaani boliye man ka aapa khoi
Auran ko sheetal karey aapahu sheetal hoi

Now I just want you *not* to listen like a dosa pan. The second method of listening is like a dew drop on a lotus leaf. You see a lotus and a dew drop on the lotus. What happens? The lotus adds beauty to the dewdrop and the dewdrop adds beauty to the lotus. They add beauty to each other. Both the beauties compliment each other and thus it becomes a beautiful feast to a painter's imagination.

Some students are like a lotus. The Master's teachings are like beautiful dewdrops. They fall on them, they are beautiful and lustrous. The moment they finish listening to a discourse and go out in the world of mundane, a gentle breeze blows and plop, the dewdrop drops away. The teaching may be beautiful. As long as you listen to the *guru*, it is fine. Once you get into mundane activities and in the process someone makes an unreasonable comment, all the teachings disappear.

The third type of student is like an oyster. Have you seen an oyster? It receives one drop of water at a particular period of time. You know what happens? One drop of water at the right point of time – only one drop and the drop becomes a pearl. The best student is like an oyster. One teaching of the master, and at the right time due to inner reflections — *mananam*, it is received like a drop. If you can be like an oyster, at the right time one drop of the teachings will take you deep within and it turns out as a pearl within you.

Lord Krishna in the *Bhagavad Gita* says, 'Even a little, Oh!

Arjuna, if you practise — *Swalpamapi asya dharmasya,* the greatest of fears will vanish — *traayate mahato bhayaat.* I invite all of you to be like an oyster. You are already in the midst of an ocean and any time may not work. Just a drop at the right time and if you keep that drop very preciously, it will create a precious stone called a pearl.

You have to make a decision now. Not just listening to my discourse, or any other discourse for that matter. Are you like a dosa pan or like a dewdrop on a lotus leaf or like an oyster? You have to make a decision. When you make a decision, that decision will go a long way in converting the teachings into beautiful seeds of understanding. Therefore, throughout, I want you to listen from your open heart. Use your heart and also your head.

The beauty of Adi Shankaracharya's unfoldment is — he has used his heart and also head. There are masters who only talk about the heart, only talk about devotion. There is no unfoldment of knowledge — *jnana,* but they only focus on devotion. There are other masters who talk about only knowledge. Adi Shankaracharya is like a union — *sangama,* of knowledge using the head, and also of poetry — *kavya,* using the heart. Both prose and poetry merge in his understanding and unfoldment.

He is also aware that he is addressing different types of people. When there is a matter related to knowledge, he unfolds with a refined language which appeals to the intellect. When there is a matter related to heart, his style of narration takes the form of poetry. In a teaching style whether it is head oriented or heart oriented, the amalgamation of both head and heart, is important. There

7

is a limitation to the knowledge based unfoldment and also there is a limitation to the heart oriented teachings.

In Indian culture, there is a maxim called *andha panku nyaaya*. The narration goes further — a blind and a lame person are trapped in a forest fire. The blind cannot see but he can walk, while the lame cannot walk but he can see. They both help each other ... lame person guiding and the blind person carrying the lame person and thus they both escape the forest fire.

I want you to feel this example. Our lives are similar to this example.

We are caught up in the forest fire of living a life of deficiency — *samsara*. Our head has one type of strength and also has one type of weakness while our heart has one type of strength and also one type of weakness. It is the blend of strengthening the strengths and weakening the weaknesses that makes a person integrated. Lord Krishna refers to such an individual as an integrated person — *yuktaha*. In such an integrated space one can come out of the forest fire of *samsara*, conflict and the chaos of ups and downs in life.

Therefore, it is necessary for us to amalgamate both head oriented knowledge and heart oriented devotion. In the words of Adi Shankaracharya, both the head and the heart should blend in right proportion. I am saying this because I want you to fine tune to this understanding. I want you to fine tune both your head and your heart right now, not only during a discourse but in all walks of your life. Dealing with your wife, sometimes only the head may not work, sometimes only the heart may not work. At times, you have to be flexible with both dimensions of your heart and head.

It is this fine tuning what is known as in management parlance the carrot and stick method. At times you have to use the carrot method and at times the stick method. You have to bring about these in combinations. The complete works of Adi Shankaracharya addresses both these methods: whether it is your head or your heart. What is very important is your commitment towards growth and enlightenment — a commitment towards enlightenment — *moksha*, towards liberation — *niravana*, call it by any name it does not matter. It is such a commitment which brings about a certain synergy, brings about certain homeostasis in your whole being.

Without commitment all knowledge one acquires will only decorate one's ego. Without commitment towards enlightenment all the feelings in one's heart are directed towards decorating a feeling that one is a very heart oriented person. Have you seen a lot of 'feeling oriented arrogance' – as some people express? More often they shun knowledge and take shelter by declaring that they are just feeling oriented.

Therefore, the bottom line is — it is neither the head oriented knowledge nor heart oriented feelings but it is the commitment towards liberation — *nirvana* which is most important.

Just for a moment let us scan back into the lives of great masters. We realise that there existed an unquenching thirst towards enlightenment irrespective of the situations or difficulties that they encountered in their lives. By studying the lives of enlightened masters one comes in touch with the recipe for engaging in an adventure — a true adventure of life.

In fact, this adventure is the very purpose of their whole life time. It is said, 'What is the quality of an enlightening person — *Siddhashya lakshanaani yani,*' should become the effort for the seeker — *saadhakasya saadhanani prayatnena sampaadyani iti shravanaat.*

For example, if someone's cooking ability is something to be emulated, the recipe of that good cooking should be taken and adopted in one's life.

Pause for a moment now. Before unfolding the *Bhaja Govindam* text, let us examine clearly our commitment and fine tune our understanding so as to get clarity and polish our understanding. All great masters had commitment towards enlightenment, and it is that commitment with which one's knowledge will sharpen the focus. One's heart, one's elevated feeling is going to smoothen one's way into the understanding. Without a deep rooted commitment nothing substantial would happen.

While engaged in a ritualistic morning and evening Vedic prayer — *Sandhyavandana* offered to invoke the Lord, one always takes a commitment — *sankalpa.* Who was Vaalmiki? He was not a very knowledgeable person, but was a simple hunter. Once when a certain transformation and understanding happened to Vaalmiki, what a person he turned out to be! He had just the mantra 'Ram' to chant with deep commitment. He followed the instructions of his *guru* and went about chanting. Even though a snake hill was built around him, he went on chanting, with the least knowledge around but with tremendous commitment. What led him to the doors of enlightenment was not the great knowledge, but it was sheer commitment.

Let us look at the life of Dhruva. As I am narrating please feel this example.

Dhruva as a young boy was distanced by his father due to the bad influence of his step-mother. When his step-brother was sitting on the lap of his father, as a child Dhruva too wanted to sit on his father's lap. The step-mother did not allow him and said, 'No, you can sit on the lap of your father only if you were born out of me.' This statement made Dhruva unhappy and he went to his mother in despair.

Dhruva's mother being a noble lady did not add fuel to fire. She did not create jealousy nor did she create anger in little Dhruva towards his step-mother.

She went about saying, 'Go and meet God. There is nothing wrong in the words of your step-mother'. That statement instilled in Dhruva a commitment to seek the higher. He moved into a forest as a child and set about meditating with a commitment that he had to come face to face with God.

Sage Narada was wandering in the forest and taking pity on little Dhruva dissuaded him from taking the harsh reality of a forest life. The great sage Narada advised, 'You know the dangers of the forest, it's not for you little one, go back to the comfort of palace and company of your mother'. Dhruva replied, 'Oh! great sage, with your blessings everything is possible. Please bless me', and he went ahead in search of the Lord.

A unique place amongst the star — *Dhruva Nakshatra* is named after him. If one studies the life of Dhruva, it is again not the possession of great knowledge but a tremendous commitment. And the mantra that he was taught to chant invoking Lord Vishnu was — *Om Namo Narayana.*

Let us take up another incident from the ancient script — *Purana.* Bhakta Prahalad did not possess a great knowledge. But his commitment was something monumental.

There are innumerable instances which I can keep quoting but the underlining fact in all these cases is nothing other than un-quenching thirst for enlightenment. Let us be inspired by noble souls in the above examples as far as commitment for enlightenment is concerned. When we start looking life with such commitment one brings a homeostasis of one's head and one's heart. It is a combination of one's head oriented understanding and heart oriented feelings that are going to bring about an inner alchemy which is beyond the realm of both head and heart.

Adi Shankaracharya with deep love and commitment invites us to seek the Lord, seek the Lord and seek the Lord, as we have sought enough here and there. I would like to draw your attention to closely watch the lineage of teacher — *guru,* disciple — *shishya,* and tradition — *parampara.* He stands out as the most outstanding teacher because of his style of addressing that includes all types of people.

That is why he is known as *Shankaram — loka Shankaram.* He covers all type of people in his unfoldment. This has been his singular most important contribution towards humanity and therefore with deep respect let us all close our eyes and bow down to the great master humbly who has devoted his whole life for bringing about this spiritual awakening.

Please open your eyes. Bring about this spiritual awakening. Let us go verse by verse and understand the unfoldment. Now don't be too caught up in your understanding of knowledge. Just feel it. Bring forth your head and also heart, and just feel the verses. Let your head be tuned towards your heart with an understanding to feel these verses from the head and the heart. I want you to first feel the verses.

VERSE 1

Does knowledge of grammar protect when death arrives?

भज गोविन्दं भज गोविन्दं
गोविन्दं भज मूढमते ।
संप्राप्ते सन्निहिते काले
न हि न हि रक्षति डुकृञ् करणे ॥
(भज-गोविन्दं... भज-गोविन्दं) (१)

Bhaja Govindam Bhaja Govindam
Govindam Bhaja Mudhamate
Samprapte Sannihite Kale
Na Hi Na Hi Raksati Dukṛn Karane
(Bhaja-Govindam Bhaja-Govindam...) (1)

भज – Seek, गोविन्दं – Govinda, भज – Seek, गोविन्दं – Govinda,
गोविन्दं – Govinda, भज – Seek, मूढमते – Oh, Foolish one!
संप्राप्ते – (When) comes, सन्निहिते – Appointed, काले – time
(death), न हि – surely never, रक्षति – protects, डुकृञ् करणे –
grammar rule, भज – Seek, गोविन्दं – Govinda

Oh, Foolish one! Seek Govinda, seek Govinda. When the appointed time comes (death), grammar rules surely will not protect you. (Seek Govinda, seek Govinda).

Let this verse sink into our hearts. Let this understanding and devotion sink into our hearts. Let the words of Adi Shankaracharya be like seeds of understanding so that the sprout of enlightenment happens.

Adi Shankaracharya unfolds, '*Bhaja Govindam, Bhaja Govindam, Govindam Bhaja mudhamate*'. *Bhaja Govindam* — seek the Lord. '*Bhaja*' means 'seek'. He is using the word all of us know of, because all of us are seeking, something or the other... seeking for power, seeking for security, seeking for pleasure, we are all seeking. Don't discard the seeking. Purify that seeking. Please understand.

I always say you don't have to discard your suffering. Make your suffering sacred. You don't have to discard your desire. Make your desire more pure, and in the purification of the very desire, you will find a different type of energy opening up. You will find desire also is a dance of the Divine and play of consciousness — *chit* vilaasam.

So the master says, *Bhaja* — literally means seek. Seek whom? He says 'seek the Lord'. You may say, 'I am seeking so many things, in the so many seeking, seeking the Lord also creates an additional tension.' When I tell people to sit in the seat of meditation, they say Swamiji, 'I have to look after my wife, my children, my growing bank balance and so on...' Now he gets a new stress called the meditation stress. Learn a mantra means a new stress called mantra stress is the expression most of the people use.

Adi Shankaracharya is inviting us to seek the Lord. When he says seek the Lord, it means seek the truth. You then find an inner understanding happening in your life, an inner awakening happening in your life. You realise the Lord is everywhere. You discover when the understanding — *jnanodaya,* takes place, the Lord is everywhere, and you find the very seeking itself is *'being there'.* In the very seeker the sought is hidden. In the very seeking itself the sought is hidden, until you discover the sought in the seeker, at least start seeking.

At present what are we seeking? We are seeking money, power, position... Yes or no? All of us definitely need more money. First thing that you ask me is — is the discourse free, or do we have to pay? Money is the first criteria for consideration. Please look deeply more out of devotion. Look into what you are seeking. In the process of seeking money, money, more money; you want more money, then you want further more money, the very more money, more money, more money is seeking what?

You are seeking for more... which in other words means you are seeking infinite. You are seeking the infinite only. If you look deeply into your seeking of money, more money, I am sure one may say having about fifty lakh of rupees, one is happy. But when you earn fifty lakh what happens? Then the target changes to hundred lakh; then a million, then a billion... It goes on and on.

Please look into yourselves very deeply. There is enough time spent on living a life in slumber. When you are looking deeply seeking more money, more power, ultimately more money, more power, you are seeking nothing but the infinite. So therefore, the great saint is inviting us to seek wisely and be wisely focused on one's seeking.

Or else you will be like a *kati patang*, neither here nor there, you will be lost. So when you are seeking more money, but deep within have this understanding that — I am seeking ultimately the infinite. When I am seeking the infinite, the infinite is nothing but the *Lord Govinda*.

The infinite is nothing but the Lord. One of the Upanishads declares, *'Esha vasyam idagum sarvam yat kinchit jagatyaam jagat'*. The Lord is indeed everywhere. Hence, Adi Shankaracharya unfolds that while seeking money one has to understand that one is seeking for the Infinite. *Bhaja Govindam, Bhaja Govindam, Govindam Bhaja mudhamate*. Oh, Fool! Seek wisely, have the right devotion. He calls *mudhamate* — Oh, Fool! It is because one's devotion can also be foolish. Have you seen some people how they demonstrate devotion; they are very devoted but very egoistic about their devotion?

Reflect on this story.

King Akbar was offering namaz, seeking the blessings from the Lord. A Sufi fakir was passing that side. He sat down waiting to ask something from the King, but when he saw that the King Akbar also was asking the Lord through his prayers, he got up and walked away. After the namaz, Akbar's attendents told him that a Sufi fakir had come to meet the King.

Akbar ordered that the Sufi fakir be traced and brought back. The King gently asked, 'What is it that you came here for?' The Sufi fakir replied, 'I came to seek something from you but when I saw you seeking something from the

Lord, I realised what one beggar can give to another beggar. I am a fakir, I am a beggar, but you are a great beggar. In fact, I beg for food, mundane worldy things, but you, the King begging for bigger things like glory, power, kingdom...'

Adi Shankaracharya questions us — what is that we are begging for? Please understand our begging can also be so foolish. He says fool — *mudhamate* because in the very devotion if one cannot discover a fulfillment, then the devotion is a means to an end. Is our devotion an extension like barter system with the Lord? 'Oh! Lord, I will do ten malas of japa, please secure me one order, and if I do twenty maalas of japa, ensure an order not only for me but also for my partner'.

Adi Shankaracharya wants us to create devotion, devotion void of any expectations. He is inviting us to a space where in the very devotion a certain fulfillment should surface. Therefore, Oh, Fool! — *Mudhamate,* I want you to understand *mudhamate* more wisely.

As I have said before, there are different types of fools. There are knowledgeable fools and there are ignorant fools. A person may be highly educated, might have obtained degrees in many disciplines or even possess a PhD, but his foolishness may still remain. I have come across many people who are very knowledgeable in different spectrum of life, but their foolishness would be dormant. What is the use of knowledge when foolishness has not gone out of their system totally? Such people are called knowledgeable fools.

There is another group of people who are not knowledgeable but are still foolish. In fact, such people are easy to deal with. Some people who are ignorant know that they are fools because they are ignorant. They may say, 'I have not read the *Bhaja Govindam* text; I do not know the *Dhakshinamoorthy stotram*...'

When one says, 'I don't know', then somebody with wisdom can help such a person, but knowledgeable fools are most difficult to deal with. Why? Because they have an illusion that they know, while they actually do not know; and if they have an illusion that they know, but in reality they do not know, then it becomes very difficult to handle such people.

Adi Shankaracharya here, is addressing a scholar who is learning grammar. He was addressing a scholar means the one who possesses a vast degree of knowledge. But he is using the word *mudhamate*, fool as a whip, as a wake up call because to call a knowledgeable person as fool — *mudhamate*, does not fit into the dictionary meaning. How can you call a knowledgeable person as fool — *mudhamate*? It is only because in this case the old man's knowledge has not destroyed his foolishness. Please understand that when one has knowledge, one's conscious mind would be clear.

Therefore in the growth of the spiritual seeker — *sadhaka,* when one is exposed to a *guru*, one may have knowledge like — I am responsible for my sorrow. Once you know you are responsible for your sorrow, and still when you get hurt, you know you are responsible for your sorrow. However, this knowledge does not totally solve the problem as ignorance does not exist in one's conscious mind. It does not exist in your conscious mind — *vyakta manaha*, but it still exists in your subconscious mind — *avyakta manaha*.

Ignorance exists in your subconscious mind. Your conscious mind has only the knowledge. In such a scenario, those who have studied and knowledgeable of the fact that they are responsible for their sorrow, will not be able to let go of their sorrow. Their foolishness does not vanish because of the knowledge that has frozen in the conscious mind.

The knowledge has not penetrated into the deeper layers of their subconscious mind. And if the knowledge has not penetrated into the deeper layers of the subconscious mind, then only your conscious mind has been lit but not your subconscious mind. But the problem exists in the subconscious mind, as you have stopped the exploration at the conscious mind.

The next obvious question would be — how to bring in a change at the subconscious level? It is the responsibility of the teacher. A teacher has to create a challenge by creating different methods in the life of a student. When faced with difficulties, we find our knowledge presents itself as, 'Why to me?' Then we start thinking. When one starts the process of thinking, one is drawing the acquired knowledge into the depth of the layers of sorrow, deep into the layers of one's conflicts and layers of one's tensions. Therefore, nature has its own method of cracking a whip. All because it wants us to explore with the knowledge that we have acquired into the subconscious and allow the subconscious mind to be cleansed.

In the case of an ignorant person he is not aware that his conscious mind is not cleansed. Thus Adi Shankaracharya says fool — *mudhamate*. When he says, 'Oh, Fool', he is respecting the knowledge that one has but now he is inviting us to take that understanding to our subconscious mind. Therefore, *Bhaja Govindam, Bhaja Govindam, Govindam Bhaja Mudhamate*.

He is also addressing the old man who is rattling out grammar sutras. It is not that grammar is *not* important, but one should know when to proceed in pursuit of a particular field of knowledge and when to stop. He says, 'Your grammar-rules are not going to protect you at the time when death arrives — *Nahi nahi rakshati dukrn karane samprapte san nihite kale*, your grammatical knowledge is not going to help you.'

In our culture there are two types of knowledge — *Vidyas*: Supreme Knowledge — *para vidya* and worldly knowledge of subjects like grammar, chemistry, biology, botany — *apara vidya*. *Apara Vidya* helps you to eliminate the superficial ignorance of the object — *toola avidya*, but it does not address the basic ignorance — *moola avidya*, the basic ignorance — *avidya* is not eliminated.

Again ignorance — *avidya* is of two types: *moola avidya* and *toola avidya*. Basic ignorance *is Moola avidya* and superficial ignorance of the objects is *toola avidya*. *Apara vidya*, the worldly knowledge will help you to eliminate the ignorance of various objects, whereas the *moola avidya* is not able to eliminate the basic ignorance.

22

Through Supreme Knowledge — *para vidya* the basic ignorance which is the ignorance of the self is eliminated.

'Nahi nahi rakshati dukrn karane'... at the time of death worldly knowledge may be useful, but it is not the true eliminator of your sorrow. Bring that understanding says the master. Hence, *Bhaja Govindam, Bhaja Govindam* — seek the truth, seek the truth, seek the Lord, because once you seek the Lord with devotion, in the very devotion itself there is fulfillment.

A lazy person cannot understand the joy of good exercise as he is rooted in the comforts of being lazy. He has not developed an understanding that engaging in good exercise regime is a joyous experience. It is unknown to him, whereas a person who is regularly engaged in exercises has developed a liking for exercising. Even if you were to ask him to be lazy he cannot, because he has discovered the joy of a healthy way of life.

Similarly, many are psychologically lazy. We have developed taste for worldly pleasures, the world of name, the world of fame, but we have not developed value for devotion and love. What is devotion? Love directed towards Truth is devotion. When we develop value for devotion as per Adi Shankaracharya, we develop value for the very love towards the Lord. When there is commitment to Truth, there is a security in one's devotion — *bhakti*, itself.

I want you to understand this. An ignorant person, who is rooted in worldly knowledge — *apara vidya*, develops security towards wealth, name, fame... He derives his

security from name, fame, wealth… but a devotee —
bhakta, knows and has the experience of devotion which
intrinsically provides him with a sense of tremendous
security. He believes that love itself is a security. When the
love itself is a security, one need not seek security
elsewhere. The true security is in devotion.

Let us look at Meera's life.

At one point of time she declared that she is wedded to
Lord Krishna even though she was married to a King.
Even when she was discarded from home, Meera with
unshakable devotion to the Lord went about singing the
name of the Lord. A woman at that period of time, and
that too from a royal family, discarded from the comforts
of a palace and going around singing the Lord's glory;
where was her security? The security was in the devotion
itself.

For example, if a person is very loving, he sees clearly that
there is fulfillment in the very love itself. Fulfillment is not
in the object of love, but in the very love itself. So, there is
security in the very love towards the Lord. That alone is a
savior — *rakshati.*

This is one of the reasons that we find from ancient times
most of the devotees — *bhaktas* are just free and wander.
They find themselves that they are most secure people in
spite of possessing nothing. They practically wander with
nothing, but they have more security, because they have
developed *bhakti ras,* the nectar of bhakti. In the very
devotion there is an intrinsic power — *shakti.* Thus a
devotee develops a different type of energy that is

uncommon as we know of.

Thus, Adi Shankaracharya declares — all these external objects, *nahi nahi rakshati*, they do not protect you, but when you have true devotion, please see, that itself protects you.

Now, an ignorant man listening to this will say, 'My God, how is it ever possible?' To them I counter ask, 'Has money ever given you security', and they say, 'Oh yes, it has given'.

I have seen in many cases — the more richer one becomes, the more one is insecure. Why more insecure?

The other person is much richer, and this track goes further and further.

I am not asking you therefore, not to work for money. Work for money, but also include 'devotion' as an addon in your life. When you develop devotion, there is an intrinsic security in the very devotion itself.

The master says, '*Bhaja Govindam, Bhaja Govindam Govindam Bhaja Mudhamate*'. Oh, Fool! – *Samprapte San nihite Kale* – at the time of death, *Nahi Nahi Rakshati Dukrn Karane* – nothing, all these are not going to protect you. What is going to protect you is the very devotion itself. How it is going to protect you? That is the mystery of devotion.

The mystery of devotion is something like this. One cannot understand poetry through prose. One cannot see the beauty of a flower through one's ears. Devotion is an *anubhava vaakya* — it is something that we have to experience ourselves. It is not an *upadesha vaakya*. It cannot be explained. It is an *anubhava vaakya*, as a matter of experience.

If it were so, why then the master is giving us *upadesha* — teaching which cannot be explained? He is only reminding us of this truth more by his presence than by his words. By his presence he is teaching. And therefore, he is teaching. Please see, once you understand this verse in totality, the fear of death starts yielding its grip over you.

Continuing further, Adi Shankaracharya unfolds the next verse.

VERSE 2

Discover the joy of detachment devoid of passion

मूढ जहीहि धनागमतृष्णां
कुरु सद्बुद्धिं मनसि वितृष्णाम् ।
यल्लभसे निजकर्मोपात्तं
वित्तं तेन विनोदय चित्तम् ।।
(भज-गोविन्दं... भज-गोविन्दं) (२)

Mudha Jahihi Dhanagamatrsnam
Kuru Sadbuddhim Manasi Vitrsnam
Yallabhase Nijakarmopattam
Vittam Tena Vinodaya Cittam
(Bhaja-Govindam Bhaja-Govindam...) (2)

मूढ – Oh foolish one, जहीहि – give up, धन आगम तृष्णां – The passion to possess wealth, कुरु – create, सद्बुद्धिं – understand reality, मनसि – in (your) mind, वितृष्णाम् – devoid of passion, यत् – with whatever, लभसे – you get, निज कर्म – by your honest actions, उपात्तं – obtained, वित्तं – the wealth, तेन – with that, विनोदय – rejoice, चित्तम् – (your) mind, भज – Seek, गोविन्दं – Govinda

Oh, Foolish one! Give up the passion to possess wealth; create in your mind devoid of passion, understand the reality. With whatever you get out of honest actions rejoice and be content. (Seek Govinda, seek Govinda).

Please close your eyes. Just close your eyes. And feel the verse from your heart. Just feel the verse from your heart.

Adi Shankaracharya says, 'Oh, *Mudha*, Oh, Fool! Do give up – *jahihi, mudha, mudha jahihi dhanagama trshnam mudha.*' Give up what? Give up the very ordinary way of living. What is it? Life lived with anxiety, striving for name and fame, the way of samsara, always anxious, always wanting. Be it in India, or abroad, be it rich, be it poor, the ordinary way is always the way full of anxieties. He says give up — *jahihi*.

Lead a life of extraordinary where in the very devotion there is security, where in the very insecurity, there is a joy. Insecurity by itself is so beautiful, because insecurity is something equal to moment to moment living. Things around us are changing, changing, changing and changing. Change is constant.

And when our hearts are filled with devotion, these changes appear as though the Lord is garlanding us with these changes. God is showering us with the gift of surprises through changes. God is inviting us to be creative and deal with fleeting moments of life, an adventure to encounter something new. The purity of our devotion gives tremendous joy.

Therefore, the master says, 'please give up — *jahihi*.' Develop the attitude of giving up and discover the joy derived out of giving up. We have, as a habit developed over the years, seek joy in asking, in taking, and in receiving. When someone gives us birthday gift, we become very happy. Look little deeper inside, we are empty. In spite of so many things that we possess we are still empty inside.

This is due to the taste that we have developed and trained to perceive that joy is only in the receiving. We have hardly developed the taste and joy of giving. We hardly give up. So he says give up — *jahihi*. In practising detachment one discovers that there is joy. It is very difficult for people to understand this concept as some even get attached to detachment. Please see this as a dangerous trap. They behave as if they are very detached. And in turn they are attached to what?

Delusion called as detachment.

I have quoted this example elsewhere too.

A teacher — *guru* accompanied by his disciple — *shishya* went out for a walk. Both had embraced monkhood. They were walking on a sea shore. They noticed a young pretty girl was drowning and seeking help. Sensing the impending danger, the *guru* dropped his water pot — *kamandalu*, and ran towards the drowning girl, picked her up and brought her ashore to safety. She was practically half naked and had almost fainted from the fear of drowning.

The *guru* helped her out and spent a few minutes to comfort her till she regained her conscious. Thereafter, the *guru* and *shisya* continued their walking. The *shisya* was a witness to all the happenings. The journey back to their abode or *ashram* took almost three hours. The *shishya* was practising silence — *mouna*. The *guru* was ready for the evening discourse.

The *shishya* asked, '*Guruji,* before you start a discourse I have a question to ask.' He continued. 'We are in a practice of observing strict code of monkhood, we have vowed to practice detachment, but you went about touching the girl who was half naked to save her. But you are forbidden to be in the company of a female. Is it not against the vow of a monkhood?'

The *guru* replied gently, 'I picked her up, saved her, and soon after dropped her thought from my mind. But you have not picked her up, but you are carrying the idea that I had picked her up not just at that moment but for so many hours in your mind. Now you tell me who is attached and who is detached?'

All this happens as one can practice things foolishly and have the illusion that one is practising things sincerely.

Therefore, please listen carefully. There is joy in detachment. Please give up attachment — *Mudhajahihi.* When I say give up attachment, I mean it is not by using force give up attachment. Have you seen people practising detachment? They shave their head, and forcefully subject themselves to many forms of physical torture to practise detachment.

If you closely observe, you notice in all those who forcefully practise detachment, a sense of innocence missing in their lives. There is no visible luster in their eyes; there is no poetry in their movement, there is no dance in their being. Why? Because, they are practising detachment not out of understanding but forcing something upon themselves. It is not by force, but out of devotion, out of a devotional understanding one has to give up. Only then, one is available to taste higher things in life.

As a kid you can afford to play, but even when you grow up also you continue to be childish, don't you? A child being childish is fine at a young age, but when he grows up and behaves like a child, it is stupid and a waste of energy. Therefore, please give away the urge for wealth because the very urge, the very greed by itself is binding — *mudha jahihi dhanaagama* is the message the great master is inviting us to look within.

Let us now turn to a famous example. I think it is from the *Panchatantra*. It enlightens us on the method employed to catch a monkey.

The monkey catcher would watch the monkeys sitting on the tree. He would carry nuts and show them to the monkeys. Then he would store the nuts in a long but narrow necked jar, leave the jar around and go away. The monkey is tempted to pick up the nuts. The monkey slides its hand into the jar through its narrow neck, takes the nuts in its fist, and tries to take the hand out. But the hand is stuck in the narrow neck of the jar. Try as hard as, it cannot pull its hand out.

As the monkey is attached to the nuts and does not want to leave the nuts, its effort turns futile. Leisurely the monkey catcher comes by whistling and catches the monkey. The monkey could have saved itself by dropping the nuts and pulling its hand out. But it is so attached and foolish that it feels it can take away the nuts easily. It pays the price because of such attachment.

But as I have told you, monkeys may now have evolved. But if you look closely, human beings have hardly evolved. They seek out to earning money, money and more money. One may be counting his days of existence, but still like the monkey in the example, one is attached to money.

Adi Shankaracharya says, 'Please bring some understanding in your life — *mudha jahihi dhanagama trsnam* but instead develop a will for detachment, develop a love for detachment — *kuru sadbuddhim manasi vitrsnam.*' This is one of the reasons when one performs offering in a sacred fire — *havan*, it is done with a feeling to focus on giving, giving and giving alone.

When once you get the joy of giving, there is a fulfillment in the very giving itself. He further adds to develop a sense of deep detachment, develop a spiritual will to give — *manasi vitrsnam*. When you develop a spiritual will to give, only then it is considered as – *yallabhase nijakarmo pattam* – whatever money that you acquire – *nijakarma* – it will be out of sincerity and honesty.

Please learn to rejoice whatever wealth you have got out of honesty and purity because only wealth earned thus is going to last – *vittam tena vinodaya cittam*.

Corruption in any society also can be minimised only when people don't take corruption as the way of life. It should be considered as sin. It never becomes an acceptable norm if the whole system is corrupted. We have, in most cases not developed the joy of being honest as a value. One's elevating attitude should be such that even if one was to earn less but one should take pride that one has earned money through rightful means or out of honest methods.

Such earnings should ring honesty in oneself which in turn leads one to fulfillment. If such a value is developed in an individual, it results in *vittam tena vinodaya cittam. Vinodaya* means learn to rejoice.

One can declare to oneself, 'I have earned this much of money by adopting honest practises'. With such honesty to the core of oneself as a value, one can learn to rejoice — *vinodaya chittam.* Thus, a celebrating mind develops in an individual. One can develop healthy tastes of earning money which is genuinely fulfilling. All other methods are just illusions.

We have to make a decision whether we want to be lost in an illusion or be floating in the reality of life. And therefore, the expression *mudha jahihi dhanagama trsnam* – not that wealth should be given up, but it is one's delusion, illusion and the infatuation towards wealth have to be given up. Once that is given up, earning wealth by no means is harmful. In fact, it can be a beautiful phenomenon. So, rejoice the value of being honest. More than wealth, rejoice the honest means, and develop higher tastes with respect to earning money.

Continuing further, as we have been seeing through these series of verses of Adi Shankaracharya's *Bhaja Govindam,* where he says, 'Oh! Fool, seek the Lord, seek the Lord.' Ultimately, it is true that we are consciously or unconsciously seeking the Lord and nothing but the Lord.

Whether one belongs to a particular religion, or one is religious or not religious, one is seeking the Lord. In the *Vedas*, the Lord is defined as the one who represents Truthfulness — *Satyam,* Knowledgeable - *Jnaanam,* Limitless Lord — *Anantam Brahma* – *anantam brahma* means limitless *Antaha na vidyate* – anything that is limitless is *anantaha* — so, therefore Adi Shankaracharya says, 'Seek the Lord', the Lord being *anantam* — limitless.

Ultimately, through money, one seeks limitlessness, through power one is seeking limitlessness, through pleasure one is seeking limitlessness. So, the bottom line is 'limitless' is what we are all seeking.

Lord Krishna in the *Bhagavad Gita* declares everybody is seeking me alone...whether one knows it or not — *mama vartma eva anuvartante partha sarvashaha*. As a spiritual aspirant one who knows that he is seeking the Lord and thus consciously direct one's seeking in a way, that give a sense of fulfillment to oneself but not a sense of deficiency. And thus the verse, — Bhaja Govindam, Bhaja Govindam, Govindam Bhaja Mudhamate.

The next verse, *mudha jahihi dhanagama trsnam* – the master says '*jahihi*' learn to give up; not give up by force, but redefine your definition of life, learn to give up your illusions of living. If we closely observe most of us are seeking illusions, whether we are conscious or not. In Sanskrit it is called as *maricha udaka nyaaya*. There is a nyaaya called as *maricha udaka nyaaya. Maricha udhaka* means mirage water. In a desert, one discovers the sight of water at a distance and so thinks water exists somewhere around. As one is drawn closer, one finds it is only a mirage and feels disappointed.

This is exactly how most of us are living our lives. We are seeking for something like a mirage. Therefore, instead of getting disappointed in life, let us learn to have an appointment with the Divine.

Seek money, there is nothing wrong in such seeking; but seek it rightfully — *nija karmopattam*; in and through your seeking money, seeking pleasure rightfully, there is no problem. While seeking, with the awareness that you are seeking the infinite, then, please see, you will not be like a person running after the mirage water. There would be no disappointment in such seeking.

In life we are disappointed not because of the world, but we are disappointed because of the illusion and delusion of the world. Please get this very clearly. People say, 'Swamiji I have renounced the world'. Why should you renounce the world? But Adi Shankaracharya says '*mudha jahihi*' — give up. Give up what? Give up the world. Can you? Where can you go if you give up the world? Even if you go to Mount Everest there is a world. Everywhere there is world. You cannot exist without world. So you cannot give up the world. You can only give up your delusion with reference to the world.

And what is the delusion? It is a conclusion that the world is the source of joy, the world is the source of security, the world is the source of happiness — *asukham imam lokam,* the Lord in the *Bhagavad Gita* says, the world is *asukham* —

has no *sukha,* means this world has no happiness. People hear this immediately and say, Oh! Yes, the world therefore has sorrow — *dukha.* Therefore, they run away from the world.

The Lord only says the world has no *sukha,* He does not say the world has *Dukha.* Sorrow — *dukha,* is a product of your illusion. For example, you crush a stone and expect mango juice. If you don't get mango juice you are angry at the stone as though the stone has brought disappointment. It's your expectation which is the problem, not a block of stone. Please get this clarity. Your expectation is the root cause of the problem and therefore you can never give up the world.

Let this understanding sink in you.

Many of you know many things. You have heard many lectures… but the problem is, if your knowing has not got the final finish of the knowing, the knowing is not going to bless you. For example, in this hall all of you are seated on the beautiful marble flooring. Such beautiful marble stone if it was not polished, it will look like simple mosaic flooring. You get marble, but you have to polish it and only then there would be shine and the luster of the Italian marble that is going to show up, isn't it? Similarly, you build a house and you finish the house neatly. Then it is livable, or else it is only 'stayable'.

Please understand this concept clearly. You have knowledge, but if the knowledge has not got the final finish, then the knowledge is only 'stayable' in your intellectual domain, but it is not really life nourishing.

Therefore, your understanding has to be nicely polished and finished. Only then it is going to bless you. And with that understanding I want you to listen further.

Hence, in the *Vedas*, it is said — *pounena shravanam kuryaat. Pounena* — constantly going on listening. For example, if you have a mirror and you don't clean the mirror often, the dust will collect on the mirror. When dust collects on the surface, your reflection is going to be very unclear. So you have to clean the mirror periodically. When the dust is removed, then the reflection is going to be clear. Similarly, our understanding has to be cleansed by proper listening as the dust of ignorance somehow settles down in the whole hustle and bustle of living life. Let this understanding be very clear because many people study *Vedanta* and they get angry with the world as if they have to run away from the world, as if they have to detach from the world. The world one cannot renounce. One can only renounce one's delusion of the world.

Now what is the basic delusion we have? The basic delusion we have is the world is going to give us happiness — *sukham*. There is a beautiful maxim — nyaaya, which says *kaaka danta anveshana nyaaya. Kaaka* means crow, *danta* means teeth, *anveshana* means searching. Most people's search for happiness is like searching or trying to count how many teeth the crow has. The crow has no teeth, but this person observing deeply with a microscope wants to count the number of teeth.

However, deep he may go into his search, it would be futile as crows do not have teeth on them. He then gets disappointed that his research has turned out to be a failure. This is called *kaaka danta anveshana nyaya.*

Similarly, the world has no happiness — *sukha,* but you have the illusion it has got happiness. When you make reality check, you find such illusion is nothing but pure delusion. Then you feel disappointed and blame the world for having given you disappointment.

One of my students was saying, 'Marriage gave me disappointment, Swamiji'. I said, 'Marriage did not give you disappointment. You expected an end, which it did not have'. This world — *loka* has no happiness — *sukha.* Thus, the whole of Adi Shankaracharya's philosophy is called *maya vaada.* You have to understand this properly, because it is most commonly misunderstood. And when the master says the world is unreal — *maya* and God alone is Truth — *Brahma Satyam Jaganmithya,* the world is *maya* means unreal not that the world is unreal. In other words the way we are looking at the world is unreal.

We project our own projected reality on the objective world. The projected reality is not in tune with the objective reality and therefore we encounter disappoint in life.

So, please get this very clearly. When we say the world is *maya,* the way we look at the world is *maya.* It is in this back drop of understanding, I want you to reflect when the master says, *'mudha jahihi'* — please give up, give up not the world, but what? *Dhanagama trsnam* — the craze for money, money and more money – you give up. So, you should not give up *dhana* — money. You don't have to give it up.

Let your intelligence and spiritual body tell you when to

give up money and when not to give up money also. Your spiritual body — *divyashareeram* will tell you and guide you when to give and when not to give. But what the master is asking us is to understand the *trsnam* — the kind of infatuation towards the wealth as we have defined wealth is going to give us joy, wealth is going to give us security... that is an illusion. Let us give away that illusion.

Kautilya, the wise in his *Artha Shastra* says earn money out of love, not out of greed. When you earn money out of greed, you experience deficiency. When you earn money out of love, an awakening of an inner expression of creativity opens up. When you earn out of love, more than the money, the very love is fulfilling. This fulfillment of the love will awaken your spiritual body that tells you at the right time what to do, when to do, and how to do?

The verse therefore is — *mudha jahihi dhanagama trsnam, kuru sadbuddhim manasi vitrsnam.* The greatest book is the book of life and how many of us really open the book of life. We all know how to read printed words; very few of us know how to read and digest unprinted words. All the books lead you through the printed words, but learn the ability to read unprinted words. This is because the greatest book is the book of one's life.

Please get this clarity. Touch yourself, touch your heart and open the book of understanding. *Swadhyayanam* means *Swasya Adhyayanam.* All these discourses should act only as a mirror — *darpana*, so you read the book of life. All my books are written concerning life. But most of us are busy in quickly following a concept, an opinion and set of dogmas and in the whole process we start becoming a philosopher analysing the logics and dynamics of words but miss the very poetry of one's living.

Continuing further, Adi Shankaracharya says,

VERSE 3

Addiction to maddening delusion and its pitfalls. Unfoldment of four disciplines of life

नारीस्तनभरनाभीदेशं
दृष्ट्वा मा गा मोहावेशम् ।
एतन्मांसवसादिविकारं
मनसि विचिन्तय वारं वारम् ।।
(भज-गोविन्दं... भज-गोविन्दं) (३)

Naaristanabharanaabhidesam
Drstva Ma Ga Mohavesam
Etanmamsavasadivikaram
Manasi Vicintaya Varam Varam
(Bhaja-Govindam Bhaja-Govindam...) (3)

नारी – of women, स्तन भर– with the weight of their breast,
नाभीदेशं – their navel, दृष्ट्वा – having seen, मा – do not, (अ) गा: –
fall a victim, मोहावेशम् – delusion covered, एतत् – this (is),
मांस – of flesh, वस – of fat, आदि – etc. विकार – a modification,
मनसि – in (your) mind, विचिन्तय – think clearly, वारं – again, वारम्
– again, भज – Seek, गोविन्दं – Govinda

*Seeing the young women's breast and navel, do not fall a victim to
maddening delusion. This is but a modification of flesh and fat.
Think clearly in your mind again and again. (Seek Govinda, seek
Govinda).*

Adi Shankaracharya started off with the verse seeking the Lord. He emphasised that don't get lost in grammar-rules, this was his first sloka. Grammar means worldly knowledge. Throughout my life, I have seen some people aged around 70 years, reading a film magazine. Invite them to a spiritual discourse, they say no time Swamiji, but for the magazine reading they have time, and so their life has become like dust bins. So, in the first verse Adi Shankaracharya has cautioned us not to get lost in the worldly knowledge.

In the second verse he went about saying *mudha jahihi dhanagama trsnam* – don't get addicted. Some people are addicted to knowledge while some are addicted to wealth. One's life is spent just acquiring wealth, wealth, more wealth. Wealth is not a problem; your infatuation towards wealth is a problem. Drop the infatuation is the essence of second sloka.

Earn money, he advises but through honest means, earn money and develop the joy of rejoicing the virtue of honesty rather than rejoicing only the wealth. People at present are rejoicing only wealth. Frankly, even wealth they cannot rejoice. Because once they have wealth, they compare with their neighbour who has more wealth than them. People define their failure by looking at someone's success. Throughout they feel they are a failure. So, the master uses *vinodaya cittam*. The word *vinodaya* is beautiful.

Learn to rejoice actions out of wise means — *nija karma*. Rejoice your honesty. One should learn this as a noble value.

A flower should enjoy being a flower; the moon should enjoy being a moon. But once you are lost in some maddening comparison, your life is going to be an unending avalanche of misery.

Now, in the third Sloka the master unfolds that when you look at someone of the opposite sex your emotions go out of control — *nari stanabhara nabhi desam*. Some people's life is wasted mainly seeking pleasure in the opposite sex. Again Adi Shankaracharya is not denouncing sex, but he only asks to bring in an understanding, bring in clarity in your pursuit. If you bring in clarity in your pursuit, then absolutely there is no problem.

Please understand that love between man and woman is an expression of natural emotion one is entitled to. Don't get lost in the attachment of the feeling. Keep the feeling and make it sacred. Only then you find you truly love your partner. Why? The male energy wants to create a completion with a female energy and vice versa. Man gets attracted to a woman; woman gets attracted to a man. In this attraction, please understand the deeper meaning where man is trying to seek completion through a woman and a woman is seeking completion through a man. And therefore, in the Indian tradition there is an emphasis on the *ardhanaareeshwara* concept.

The idol of *Ardhanaareeshwara* represents half *Shiva*, the male and half *Parvati*, the female that denotes both the male energy and the female energy that are beautifully balanced and harmonised. For example, you and I are born from our parents. We are a product of our parents both male and female energies. We have to only balance it properly. Elsewhere, in some of my other books and talks I have quoted how to balance the male and female energy; but I am only trying to explain why we are attracted to opposites. I have referred to this even in a simple discourse. If I find the majority during my discourse are only men, I can feel the energy level that is different. And the same is true if the majority of the group consisting women. It is in the right combination of male and female, one finds the audience vibrant. As a speaker, I do feel so...what to talk about energies within you.

So please understand that throughout existence men are seeking women, and women are seeking men. In fact, we try to seek completion through this and hence attraction to opposites.

Now you have to bring in a little more understanding. The attraction to love a man or a woman is based on what? Is it just one's physical body? Or is it something beyond a body that one really loves? Elsewhere, Adi Shankaracharya is going to say that we do not really love the body because when breath — *praana*, the life force — *jeeva shakti*, goes away, not even one night one can sleep with one's spouse — *tasyaam bharye bibbhyati kaaye*. Please understand this very clearly.

Therefore, one is not seeking a man or a woman, but one is seeking the energy behind the man and the woman.

One can observe similar phenomenon even among a simple plant which is naturally grown and artificially tendered. When touched an artificial plant, one does not feel the naturalness that is associated with the pleasant feeling of such experience. In fact, subsequently, one may even not feel like touching it again. But the story is different with respect to naturally grown plant. One may feel a repetitive urge like touching again and again as it has life. Artificial plant may appear equally pleasing as a natural plant, but it has no life.

Similarly, within you and me there is life energy — *jeeva shakti*. There is a Divine energy — *divya shakti*. Relationship should be connected to Divine energy — *divya shakti*. Respect the body but don't stop at that. Stopping at the bodily level has to be denounced. Then the relationship goes little deeper which helps one to see the source. Having discovered a source you respect the body. There is, absolutely no problem in such case.

So it is that attitude of stopping at the body, and not going deeper beyond the body is what is to be denounced.

Our scriptures dwell deeply on four disciplines — *shastras,* namely *dharma, artha, kaama* and *moksha.* All of these have to be understood deeply in order to dicepher what Adi Shankaracharya is dwelling.

For example, *kaama shastra* does not simply describe sex or indulgence. The whole *kaama shastra's* focus is to convert *maithuna* into *prarthana* — converting one's sexual act into a form of a prayer. When one converts one's sexual act into a prayer, one is not stopping at the body. Body is alive and vibrant because of Divine power — *divya shakti* and that is why one goes deeper into the sexual act.

The second aspect in the *kaama shastra* dwells on a man and a woman's relationship where the energies of *kaama* should be used for progeny – *santaanam*. Directing sexual energy for progeny helps one coming in contact with Divine energy and at the same time one is disciplining the sexual energy. This understanding helps in disciplining one's desire and lead to harness the rogue elephant *kaama*, the burning sexual desire. Like how a rogue elephant if not tamed, creates chaos all round; so too, one's *kaama* if not tamed, can create chaos. So the *kaama* needs to be harnessed and channelised to a purpose.

The significance of marriage and relationship with a single partner leads one to a disciplined endevour where the wild burning sexual desire — *kaama* is channelised as a tamed elephant, or else one's sexual life could turn out to be wild and scattered.

Reflect on this story that I recently came across.

Mullah Nazruddin, one of the Sufi characters used to greet and compliment every woman he came across as, 'You are the best and also you are the most beautiful woman'. When asked by his wife what made him consider every woman as the most beautiful, Mullah replied, 'What can I do? Every woman I meet appears more beautiful than the earlier woman I have met. Each woman is better than the best.'

One can play with words; each woman is better than the best. Thus one's whole life revolves around chasing women.

Kaama shastra's discipline is to make one's *kaama* sacred and at the same time discipline one's sexual energy in a relationship. While taming the energy in a relationship, the scattered, wild and licentious energies gets converted into a commitment and therefore, the vow of seven sacred steps of rituals that are undertaken by the couple — *saptapadi*, becomes an important milestone in cementing a committed relationship of marriage. Such relationship with understanding runs deep in the exploration of two individuals.

Thus, *kaama shastra* emphasise one to convert the sexual act into a prayer — *maithuna* into *praarthana*, and by using it to procreate in a sacred space.

Dharma Shastra says — the foundation of one's life governing principle should be on the basis of righteous living — *dharma*. Out of *dharma* let us earn money and out of such earnings, let us undertake the path of service — *seva*. It is said, 'Serving people is serving God — *Nara seva* is *Narayana seva*'. *Dharma* should be followed not for the sake of acquiring virtue — *punya* to go to heaven — *vaikunta*. The purpose of *Dharma* is — let actions emerge from basic premise of goodness. Out of such goodness principle, let us earn money.

Artha Shastra emphasis — earn money out of love and not out of greed. The whole *artha shastra* focuses on earning money out of love. It summarises that it is beautiful to earn money out of love. If earned out of greed, one loses both the balance and direction.

Moksha Shastra sets a goal about how one can convert inner deficiency — *samsara*, into inner fulfillment —

nirvana. How one's *samsara* itself can become a point of *nirvana*, how one can be free in *samsara* and not creating conflict with *samsara* is the edifice of a wonderful life nourishing philosophy.

If we can understand and live in *samsara* in the right way, then every experience will be a teacher. We must convert every experience as an opportunity to learn. Lord Krishna, in the *Bhagavad Gita* says, '*Sama dukka sukham dheeram saha amritatvaaya kalpate*'. All through your joy — *sukha*, your sorrow — *dukkha*, your achievements — *labha,* your losses — *alaabha*, let there be equanimity — *samabhavana*. Your sorrow — *dukka* is teaching you something, your happiness — *sukha,* is teaching you something, your achievement — *siddhi* is teaching you something, loss — *asiddhi,* is teaching you something, people's blame — *ninda,* is teaching you something, everything is teaching you something and this is what *moksha shaastra* talks about in detail.

These are four pillars namely *the dharma, artha, kaama and the moksha shaastras*. With understanding drawn from all of them, if one were to love a woman, or love a man, one is not blown away by the love. Instead one grows in such love. One will not fall in love, but one will rise in love.

People often say, 'I fell in love, Swamiji what shall I do?' 'Fall often and that too deep', I say. 'Who told you to fall in love? A ladder is meant for going up and why are you going down. Love is meant for you to go up'.

Now with this clarity, with this vision please reflect the verse, *nari stana bhara nabhi desham*. When you look at the breast of a woman, don't get carried away and lose your sanity, the master emphasises. He is saying very lovingly to look at the reality, *nari stana bhara nabhi desham drishtva magha moha vesham* — don't get lost. *Ye etat mamsa vasadi vikaram* — the body is nothing but only flesh — *maamsa*, only meat.

Somebody interpreted it saying – therefore, hate it. It is not that you have to hate it; you are also born out of your parents only. It is only a modification of flesh. Are you in love with the modification of the flesh or do you love the force behind the flesh? Because you have not seen the force, you are just carried away. Overnight this understanding will not dawn upon. But constantly one has to, think over — *manasi vichintaya* on and on — *varam varam.*

Sanskrit is such a beautiful language. *Samyak kritam* is called *samskritam*. Samskritam means *samyak* — very well, *kritam* very well done, it is a very spiritual language.

For example, the word *kaama* has a meaning for desire; *kaama* is also a meaning for lust or sex. The word *kaama* has both the meanings. One can employ the word for desire, one can also use the word to convey sex, and also it can be used to depict lust. Please look at why is it so? *Kaama* not only refers to the emotion between man and woman, *kaama* also means desire. Isn't it? *So kaamayata bahusyaam prajaayeti,* the Lord desired, 'Let me have many…' So *kaama* means simple desire, but the meaning as we understand is sex and lust also. Both are fine and it does not matter.

Some people may not have *kaama* for man or woman, some have *kaama* for money.

I saw something wonderful recently. I was in Las Vegas and came across a funny card. They have inserted a naked woman's picture in between the playing cards. Many psychologists may have put their mind into this strange happening... where a plain card of a naked woman is inserted between a set of playing cards. When one sees someone naked, suddenly eyes pop out with an uncanny expression.

Same energy overflows in many, but for some people even when they look at money also their eyes pop out. In case of someone like politicians power means, 'Oh! I will aspire to be a minister, I will become prime minister.' It does not matter whether *kaama* is towards fulfilling sexual desire; *kaama* is towards earning more money or acquiring more power. It is ultimately different versions of the basic essence.

What our Rishis want us to see is — whenever we are in the spell of a desire — *kaama*, when desire arises in us and if we can convert it into a point of enlightenment — *moksha*, that is true awakening. Let us forget about the object of desire — *kaama*, but can we just look at the energy that is moving. When *kaama* arises, be it in the name, money, power... as is in the case of *tantric* practice, it is said don't look at the object of desire but look at the movement of desire. When we look at the movement of desire, we come across that the movement of desire is nothing but energy, energy, and flow of energies.

And when we start experiencing, flowing and melting with such energies, the object becomes less important. What is more important is movement of energies. In such a space of understanding desire — *kaama* does not create any problem in an individual.

Kaama creates a problem whenever we miss seeing the Divine energy which is flowing in us but instead when we focus only on the object of the energy. When we see the object of desire, we miss the Divine force of the play of consciousness — *chit vilaasa,* which is happening inside us. In certain tantric practices, one is advised to lead one's beloved on one's lap, closing eyes and watching the flow of energies that are moving and start experiencing only the experience of such energies without naming and wording the experience.

Similar practice is followed when you are looking at a plant. For example now look at a plant afresh. When you look at a plant, you are trained yourself to see the form, to see the color, to see the combination of leaves... as the case may be. In tantric practice, it is suggested to see the plant without a form... and it goes into finer aspects from there on. When you see a tantric, you notice instantly their eyes. Their eyes are very powerful. But you are trained yourself to look at the form. How can you look at a plant without a form? How can you look?

Please notice that there is a formless presence; the energy which is moving and the vibration of the plant has no form. But you are used to seeing the form, but the plant is alive because of certain energies that are formless. There is a certain kind of fragrance which is generated around it and that too has no form. And if you start noticing at the energy, the fragrance and the presence of a plant, you are training yourself to see the formless in a form.

The Upanishad declares, *Ashariram* means no body, *sharireshu*, in this body. In the body which has a form — *shariram*, our Rishis say as *ashariram* — there is something without body, which in turn means formless. There is a formless in the form. That is why I named this *ashram* as *Nirguna Mandir*. *Nirguna* means no form. This is based on purely a tantric concept. If you closely see, it is in the shape of a womb; further, as we all know the mother's womb is the most secure place to be in. You and I have spent good many months in our mother's womb and when we are born we always look out for the security like our mother's womb. And enlightenment — *moksha*, is the greatest security.

Please understand this concept clearly. We are trained ourselves to look at a form. We have not trained ourselves to look at formless. Therefore, the invitation is to look for formless in the form. Look at the bodilessness in the body. So when *kaama* arises, our Rishis wants us not to get lost in the object of desire but to focus on the movement of the energies that is formless. The movement itself is a play of consciousness — *chit vilaasa*. If you can taste that movement in totality, you will find that you are nothing but a flow, rather than a destination. Life is not a destination. It is a flow from moment to moment to moment.

We try to convert life into a destination as we are comfortable with something that is well defined. We are not comfortable with something that is undefined.

Therefore, with this understanding, *nari stanabhara nabhi desham, drishtva magha mohavesham* — when you look at the breast of a woman, don't get carried away and lose your sanity, look at the reality, don't get lost, *etat mamsa vasadi vikaram* — this body is only a flesh — *mamsa, manasi vichintaya* — think over deeply, *vaaram vaaram*, again and again, because overnight this understanding will not happen.

Kabir, in one of his famed quotes mentions,

> *dheere dheere re manaa dheere sab kuch hoi.*
> *Mali seechai sou ghada ritu aaye phal hoi.*

Slowly things will happen. Therefore, this understanding should be constantly reflected upon. When this understanding is reflected upon constantly, we find our life is a great awakening.

We try to understand in our own language the many words of enlightened masters. We don't try to understand the unknown wisdom the master is standing for. We try to understand the master from the knowledge that we know. The knowledge that we know, is nothing but ignorance masquerading as knowledge.

The master is able to identify our own language and also is aware of the fact that our known knowledge has not blessed us very much. Therefore, he takes our own language and with the words which we know, he is giving a meaning, which we do not know. That is the greatest task of teaching. For example, if I start talking in Gujarati and you know only Punjabi, then nothing is understood by you. For some people nothing is understood anyway inspite of attending many discourses.

A *guru* has to talk about something profound which is beyond in the realm of language. But we don't understand that language. What should he do? He has to take our language, which we know, our language that he knows and through our language, which we know, give a meaning to that profundity that we don't know. What happens then? We drop our words and start seeing a meaning, which is beyond words.

The Upanishad says, *'Yatho vaacho nivartante apraapya manasa sahaa'* — words tried to unfold the truth and but words returned unsuccessfully...

Words tried to convey the truth but could not. Therefore, we have to be very clear. Words cannot contain the truth. *Manasi vichintaya vaaram vaaram*, reflect on this constantly. If we superficially understand, we will understand as a discard woman or a discard man. It is not so.

In Rishikesh my *guru* used to give an example. There was a *sadhu*. Every time a woman walked past him, he used to cover his face with his book. He never looked at any woman because of his understanding that he would get polluted if he were to see a woman. My *guru* used to humorously narrate that throughout he would be thinking mentally that he should have seen at least what dress a woman was wearing. That is not the way to get out of it.

There is a spiritual organization where they advise the participant that if you get married and are having a relationship with your wife, your atma would get polluted. This organization has a massive following is another mystery around us.

One of my students whose would-be wife works in that particular spiritual organization came to me with a predicament. He was to get married to that lady but the question was — the moment he touches her she would say to herself that her atma gets polluted. 'Swamiji, what to do?' was his burning question. I called for the lady and she narrated the same. I asked her how can her atma get polluted when her would-be husband touches her? I am telling you that she was trying to convince me how her atma gets polluted in such a case.

I had to tell her that she was a product of such pollution. Where is the question of further pollution? Such foolishness you find in people and they have a massive following. I suppose one can talk foolishly about anything and get a massive following, but on the other hand talk wisely you get less following.

Adi Shankaracharya says don't get carried away by the sight of a woman's breast. He says — understand the body is only a form of a flesh. What is the life behind the body? Elsewhere, in a verse he is going to unfold that if life goes, can you be with your beloved even for one night?

Therefore, with this understanding be in a relationship. When you are in a relationship with this understanding your vision is not short sighted, but in fact your vision will be much deeper. When it is deeper, life then becomes fulfilling. Your partner is only a window to the sky of a sacred space — c*hidambaram*. In such a space a different understanding altogether opens up. Is it clear?

Now continuing further, the next verse goes as,

VERSE 4

What is the key to inner freedom?

नलिनीदलगतजलमतितरलं
तद्वज्जीवितमतिशयचपलम् ।
विध्दि व्याध्यभिमानग्रस्तम्
लोकं शोकहतं च समस्तम्
(भज-गोविन्दं... भज-गोविन्दं) (४)

Nalinidalagatajalamatitaralam
Tadvajjivitamatisayacapalam
Viddhi Vyadhyabhimanagrastam
Lokam Sokahatam Ca Samastam
(Bhaja-Govindam Bhaja-Govindam...) (4)

नलिनीदलगतजलं – the water (drop) resting on a lotus petal (is),
अति – very, तरलं – uncertain (existence), तद्वत् – so, जीवितं – life,
अतिशय – ever (greately), चपलम् – unstable, विध्दि – understand,
व्याधि अभिमान ग्रस्तं – caught by disease and pride, लोकं – the
world, शोक – with sadness, हतं – is (filled), च – and,
समस्तम् – whole, भज – Seek, गोविन्दं – Govinda

The water drop resting on a lotus petal has a very uncertain existence; so also is life ever unstable. Understand the very world is caught by disease and pride and is filled with sadness. (Seek Govinda, seek Govinda).

Please feel what is being said now.

Use your head, use your heart, close your eyes, feel, and feel what is being said. With deep love in your heart just feel, feel from your heart.

Nalini dala gata jala mati taralam tadva jivitam atishaya chapalam — life is transitory. Please understand, people listen to all this and conclude, 'Swamiji, thank you very much. I did listen nicely, but practice? I'll do in the next birth.'

For example, people offer full body prostration out of respect — *sashtang namaskara*. When you offer *namaskara* your ignorance has to be dropped. Listening to everything but practising during next birth means not willing to give up ignorance. Amongst Hindus there seems to be no hurry at all as they believe in many births. In other religion the belief system is that there is one lifetime, so one has to complete all spiritual accomplishment on a fast track.

Most Hindus are immunized to the philosophy of *punarapi jananam, punarapi maranam, punarapi janani jatare shayanam* — many lives are there in the cycle of unending life and death, so one is highly relaxed. One of the plus points of this understanding is that they are very relaxed and the more you go to certain towns you find people are more relaxed.

One of my books in Tamil *'Manase Relax Please!'*, was released in Madurai city. We were driving a car. There was a cyclist who was crossing from one side of the road to the other side. He neither looked left side nor right side, but just crossed. The car was at a good speed and so had to brake suddenly, and what a sound it created. I did not want to see what happened, but to my utter shock the cyclist simply went on as if nothing had happened. I said, 'Manase (mind) relax' but the essence of the book may not be a necessary for someone in Madurai city as there is a different kind of problem. People seem to be over relaxed. I am not joking; I expected that at least he will turn back and see what had happened.

This could be one of the reasons why Westerners coming to India are so tensed especially with respect to our traffic order. Every vehicle in the chaotic traffic is a moment to moment death for them. For us nothing happens, a speeding lorry passes, someone dies and no problem... as the next birth is there in any case.

The deep rooted psyche justifies that the same idiot is going to get married in the next birth also and thus one takes the spouse for granted and life thus goes on.

So here, the master says — please understand this practice, this *vidya*, and practice it right now. What is life? *Nalini dala gata jala mati taralam tadva jivitam atishaya chapalam* – life is transitory. Life is like a dewdrop on a lotus. A dewdrop looks so beautiful on a lotus flower.

Do you know why in India, a lotus flower is called as the queen of all flowers? The lotus grows in muddy water. Symbolically all Gods are seated on lotus, do you know why? It grows only in muddy water, as in very clean water it may not grow. Then a certain secretion takes place on it. When water is poured on a lotus it does not get really wet but like a diamond the dewdrop will be dancing.

In life too, we have to grow from muddy water

circumstances. Thus, do not expect an ideal life. No ideal husband, no ideal wife, no ideal *guru* also. Everybody is a personification of many pluses and minuses. Don't nurse such delusions of perfection.

As a lotus that grows in muddy water and yet not affected by its surroundings, one's growth parameter should be unruffled against all odds such as bad influence of external situations, disappointments, extreme difficulties, or entrapment of muddy surroundings of life. Lotus is like a symbol that invites us to scale a new height in our daily living. That is why Adi Shankaracharya uses it as a symbol, where traditionally lotus is well known for its unique quality. Now, we do not know that, is a different matter altogether.

Most of those who sport a symbolic marking on the forehead — *naama,* and they don't know the deeper meaning of it. Some even say it is only for decoration. For example, how can ash — *vibhuti,* smeared on one's forehead be termed as decoration? Please understand ash — *vibhuti* that smeared on one's forehead carries a deeper meaning of life.

Ultimately, it represents that one's body is going to be reduced to ash — *vibhuti.* So every day when someone applies *vibhuti* on one's forehead, it is to remind oneself that ultimately one's body will turn into ash. Do not cultivate infatuation towards body, but start learning to live beyond your body.

In India, it is a custom among the majority women to put on a traditional mark, a *bindu* on their forehead. I have seen some of my students who sport a *bindi*. Their dressing mirror is filled with various designs of them. I asked someone about its source and was told that fancy shops display hundreds of varieties.

Again, please understand that one does not put it on just for decoration. It is a constant reminder to oneself to facilitate opening of the third eye or intuitive centre in oneself. The message is — don't look at life with ordinary eyes; look at life from a spiritual eye. That is the meaning. All this is forgotten. But we have to remind ourselves again and again. Similarly, a lotus is referred as a symbol as it is well known in Indian culture.

If you closely see, life is like a dewdrop on a lotus leaf and thereby indirectly telling us to rise from muddy water surroundings to bloom into a queen of flowers. That is the hidden message.

Again, like how a lotus is unaffected by dewdrops on lotus leaves, don't get affected by situations of life. Develop that secretion in you; develop that knowledge — *vidya* in you. When you have devotion — *bhakti*, nothing is going to happen to you. When you acquire wisdom — *jnana* and devotion — *bhakti*, nothing is going to affect you. So providing indirectly these symbolic meanings to life is to equip one by conveying the deeper message — that one's life is transitory.

Now, all of us have heard this. But when we live life, do we live life as transitory? We live life, for example on the assumptions that, 'Yes, my horoscope clearly shows Swamiji that I will live for 75 years'. But the astrologer who predicted may not have predicted his life span and he would have been dead and gone. 'It is clearly written in my horoscope' one may justify.

Similarly, we know this only as a concept that our life is transitory, but are we living life, as if life is transitory? Knowledge has to percolate into behaviour. Knowledge has to percolate in the movement of action, not in the lip movement in form of a discourse. If you elevate yourself and start living life with this understanding that life is transitory, every moment you are going to be complete and total. Who knows the very next moment may not exist at all!

Reflect on this.

One of my students' spouse is young, hale and healthy; she was undertaking a tour to north Indian cities. During the tour her husband spent more time than required in the bathroom. She called on him many times, but no response. 'How long are you taking?' She yelled at him. Generally people relax in a bathroom. It appears as best place for relaxation. I can't understand how people read papers, magazines... in the comfort of a bathroom! I am not sure if the fragrance in a bathroom is so inviting and intoxicating! Else why would one use bathroom for reading purpose?

In this case she ran out of patience as her husband was just not responding to her repeated calls. Sensing danger, they had to call on the other members of the family and had to break open the door. And they found him dead due to a massive heart attack. He had not subjected himself to routine medical check up as he was operating with an understanding that he was hale and healthy. He had attended one of my workshops and I knew him.

His wife regrets and mentions, 'I know Swamiji, it sounds true when you say life is transitory. Before this incident, I was just listening to your discourse that life is transitory.

Sometimes, when a *guru* teaches you, you don't really understand. Some even abuse the teachings. When you are abusing the teaching of a master, nature has its own method to teach you the understanding. This is what is called as 'unconscious shock'. You give a conscious shock and get the word meaning, but nature out of infinite compassion gives you an 'unconscious shock' because it warns and wants you to grow, and grow sensibly.

I can narrate through several examples. In spite of it, if one's ignorance — *ajnana,* is deep rooted and strong, one feels one would live for several years without any health issues. For the sake of saying as a party talk, we may say, 'Anytime we can die', but our gut level feeling says silently, 'another 30 years', and when those 30 years have passed, we may still say to ourselves internally, 'another 30 years'. I am not saying that you don't be positive, but I want you to live life in a way as if this is the only moment available. If you can truly know that the only moment available is 'now', you will truly love this moment, truly rejoice this moment and contribute goodness to the moment. Whatever good be present, it is in that moment and in that very recognizing and rejoicing you find the Lord dancing in the very moment.

Most of us are never total to the present. We are either dissatisfied of the past or distasteful to the present, distrust the future, and thus it goes on...

Adi Shankaracharya says, '*nalini dala gata jala mati taralam tadvad jivitam atishaya chapalam* — please understand not only in conscious mind, but let us go deep into the subconscious mind — *avyaktamanha*, as our ignorance exists in our subconscious mind also, *viddi vyadhyabhimana grastam,* one's body is full of disease — *vyaadhi.*

Just to give you an example, if we were to see our own palms under microscope, we see them with full of bacteria. We are actually in the space of emergency, anytime anything can happen. It appears that we are moving only in an emergency van, anything can strike at anytime.

Geographically also, if you see the surface below the earth, there are several heat bodies due to fire movement. Anything can happen anytime. Above this space it is said asteroids are moving, and below is like a heated oven. That is why volcanoes erupt from down under; actually there is hot lava down below and above we have asteroids moving. They say if one of the asteroids crashes into earth's space and the effect could be destruction of an entire city of the size of Bangalore City. Mysteriously, these forces are balanced.

So, above the sky asteroids are moving, below the earth surface it is like a hot oven and in between we have mosquitoes and other deadly viruses, some identified while others have still escaped medical scrutiny that can inflict variety of diseases. We are living a life that is full of uncertainties and still we have an illusion of living a permanent life.

Not only here but in heaven also, we feel we would live eternally. If life in this world itself is not permanent, how will life in heaven be permanent?

How can one be permanent anywhere? In fact, if you are making an entry into heaven so there should be an exit too. What is born has to die — *Jaatasya hi dhruvo mrituhu*. When your results of good deeds – *punya* gets over, it is your turn to head back where you started from — *Ksheene punye martyalokam vishanti...*

Please see, *viddhi vyadhyabhimana grastam, lokam soka hatham ca samastam* – and understand you are expecting the world to be joyful, and because you expect the world to be joyful, it is *shokam*, the world is sorrow. Why is it so? Because you expect the world will provide you joy. The world has to offer neither joy nor unhappiness. It is your expectation that brings you disappointment. And, therefore the verse, *soka hatham ca samastam*, whole world is riddled with sorrow.

For instance, you come to me and expect me to give you a sweet, a *laddu* in return. People say this Swamiji is very different, he doesn't give *laddus* or *boondis* and he doesn't perform magic. One person expected me to do that and went out very disappointed, because he thought some magic will take place through me.

I said, 'You are the greatest magic. In spite of under-standing you still have the misunderstanding of what I have been unfolding. In spite of knowledge you continue to be stupid'. Please see that here is a person disappointed because he expects a *guru* to be like his definition of a *guru*.

Therefore, his sorrow is not because I gave him sorrow, he expected something other than what I gave. I am giving understanding, I am giving clarity. What he wants is how to increase his bank balance and so on.

A few days back somebody came to me and said, 'I am losing hair fast, is there any mantra by which my hair can come back'. I said because of mantra my hairline is receding. God has infinite wisdom. Hair fall means so many unnecessary things are dropping...

One person preserved carefully all his fallen hair. You think I am joking. One of my students has preserved it. It is due to attachment to one's own hair. There are so many other things falling or are coming out of your system. If you were to preserve all those silly things what would be the state of your house.

So therefore, life is temporary — *lokam soka hatham cha samastham*. So be very total. Life is total. Every moment live in totality with joy. The very seeking itself gives you tremendous joy. Thus, *Bhaja govindam, bhaja govindam, govindam bhaja mudhamate*. Seek the Lord. *Samprapte sannihite kale nahi nahi rakshati dukram karane*.

Elsewhere the master says, '*Ka te kanta kaste putrah samsaro yamativa vicitrah* – who is your wife, who are your children, don't start depending on them and make your life miserable, love them but have this clarity.'

Let us continue further. We saw in the few classes that there is an understanding which emerges from the mind, there is an understanding which emerges from the heart, and there is an understanding which emerges from the synergy of both head and the heart.

Thus, cleansing one's thinking and mind is *vichara shuddhi*, cleansing one's feeling is *bhava shuddhi* and when these two cleansings — *shuddhis* are merged together it turns out to be *atma shuddhi*. In such a space, one finds a different type of understanding opens.

When you understand from the level of mind there is one level of understanding. It is like knowing half the truth. But it is a combination of the head and heart where a synthesis has to emerge and in such emergence of both we find a different energy of understanding starts occurring. Then we find the depth of our perception is very cognitive and hence very holistic. Adi Shankaracharya is unfolding this in very many different ways and dimensions.

Continuing further he says.

VERSE 5

Difference between attachment and caring for kith and kin

यावद्वित्तोपार्जनसक्ता
स्तावन्निजपरिवारो रक्त: ।
पश्चाज्जीवति जर्जरदेहे
वार्तां कोऽपि न पृच्छति गेहे ।।
(भज-गोविन्दं... भज-गोविन्दं) (५)

Yavadvittoparjanasakta
Stavannijaparivaro Raktah
Pascajjivati Jarjaradehe
Vartam Kopi Na Prchhati gehe
(Bhaja-Govindam Bhaja-Govindam...) (5)

यावत् – as long as, वित्त – of wealth, उपार्जन – to earn, सक्त: – has the capability, तावत् – so long, निजपरिवार: – your kith and kin, रक्त: – attached (to you), पश्चात् – afterwards (later on), जीवति – lives (comes to live), जर्जर – infirm, देहे – body, वार्तां – word, कोऽपि – anyone, न – not, पृच्छति – oh, cares to asks, गेहे – at home, भज – Seek, गोविन्दं – Govinda

As long as there is the capability to earn, so long the kith and kin are attached to you. Later on, when you come to live with an infirm body no one at home cares to speak even a word with you. (Seek Govinda, seek Govinda).

All of us like it or not, do have psychologically ignorant deposits in our being. Just like some people have fat deposited at one part in their body, for some people fat gets deposited at another part, for some other people fat gets deposited at many parts of the body. So also, there are ignorant pockets in us which get deposited and distributed in different areas. Therefore, the *guru*'s task is to eliminate those ignorant points.

This is something related to one's exercise regime. There is an overall exercise that one focuses on. There is also a spot reduction that one works on. Overall exercising, like walking will not work on certain special or critical areas. Similarly, one should recognize one's ignorance has so many psychological points and if those points are not eliminated, they start interfering into the very perception of what one has perceived.

In the first verse Shankaracharya says — don't get lost in knowledge. In the second verse, he talked about — don't get lost in your infatuation to money. Then he says, *'nari stanabhara nabhi desam'* — when you love somebody, don't get lost, don't fall in love with the window and thereby miss the sky. So the body is like a window; respect the window called body. Don't limit yourself to the body because behind the body there is a soul that you need to recognize. In English there is an expression called soul mates — which means you and I have to be soul mates.

The master went step by step and in this verse, he says, please have clarity. He's just giving the clarity. Once you have the clarity, like when you have light at your disposal, wherever darkness may be, take the light and the darkness disappears and dispelled. Please see it is not something you like or dislike. Our whole understanding in life is, 'I like this'. Opposite of like is dislike. That is what the master is saying. Just have this clarity.

He says, '*Yavad vittoparjana sakta.*' He wants to create detachment — *vyragya,* in us. Detachment is a tremendous inner freedom. So he says — *yaavad vittopaarjana saktaha* — understand that reality bites. Therefore, so long as there is wealth, you find people are connected to you.

How? *Stavannijaparivaro raktah* – then your family — *parivaro,* is around you so long as you have wealth. He then says, '*Pascajjivati Jarjaradehe*' – when you start getting older and older then slowly they start moving away from you. Then he further adds, '*Vartam kopi na prcchati gehe* — when you become old nobody even asks how you are. A nuisance value you become – *vartam kopi na prcchati gehe.* As you get older people don't bother much about you, but if your family happens to be a very enlightened family, it gives more respect to the older member. That is a different matter prevalent even today in some of the families. But he is addressing ordinary people — *saamanya jana,* general category of people and how they are, the worldly people and how they are. Therefore, don't have undue attachment.

There is a difference between attachment and caring. Care for your body, don't be attached to your body; care your family, but don't be attached to your family. The moment you care, you will contribute; the moment you care, you will connect wisely. The moment you are attached, your subject gets superimposed on the object. Attachment speaks of your qualities that you nourish; attachment speaks of the lower center in you. Caring speaks of the higher centers in you. The lower center operates from attachment while the higher center operates from caring energy.

So therefore, please see — so long as there is wealth, people are going to ask about your welfare, the family will be hovering around you, this is the order of the ordinary world — *saamanya loka,* and you do find people are out there for you. But once the wealth diminishes and as you start getting old *vartam kopi na prcchati gehe,* your own people at home will not bother to ask you how you are. Therefore understand people, who are in love with you, are more in love with the position that you are in. More than you, people love the wealth that you have. This is the ordinary way, not everybody is like that.

There is a very beautiful Sufi story I am reminded of now – A King invited a Sufi mystic for a dinner. The King was waiting for him at the dining table along with the other invitees who were great scholars. The Sufi mystic presented himself in ordinary casual attire. Looking at his attire and not recognizing who he really was, the watchmen and other guards of the palace did not allow him inside. The Sufi mystic then returned with appropriate attire and was allowed an entry into the palace. Once seated on the dining table, he removed his coat and kept it next to him on a chair. When food was served, he offered it to the coat. This appeared ridiculous.

Such a wise person indulging in a silly act drew the

attention of everyone present. The King intervened and asked, 'Why are you offering food to the coat and what is the reason for your silly act?' The Sufi mystic answered, 'I was allowed inside only because I wore this coat, so therefore people are recognizing the coat, and food is served to the coat and not to me.'

How many of us see things as they are? We see the position of the person. We see the wealth that one has. How many of us are really respecting one's commitment, the service, and the love? This does not mean to say that if a person has a respectable position one need to disrespect him, but have the clarity. When you have clarity, you demonstrate caring energy and you will not have energy of attachment.

Have you observed that the first thing a priest does when you go to a temple to offer *pooja?* He makes you take a commitment — *sankalpa* and then make you chant — *jnaana bhakti vyragya siddhyartham aham idam poojaam karishye.* Meaning 'I am performing this pooja just to get understanding — *jnana,* devotion — *bhakti,* and detachment — *vyraagya.* I am doing the pooja to get these three important aspects of life including detachment.' Detachment creates great liberation in an individual. Absence of such clarity, leads one into a life of misery.

Adi Shankaracharya, with his paintbrush of words and feelings, is trying to create in us a great sense of detachment that in turn would bring out objectivity.

Reflect on this story.

A father was very attached to his children. When his wife died, he had to take up the responsibility of nursing the children in a dual role of a parent. Children were showing up as irresponsible during their growing years. The father, out of sheer love and his attachment started giving more attention to his children to make up for their irresponsibility. This continued till his old age. The more he looked after them with care, more irresponsible these children were turning out.

While 'taking good care of children', one must see clearly if they are becoming irresponsible. Sometimes 'not looking after' may be a better option. Children may become responsible for their life. Or else they may squarely put the onus on the parents to look after their lives.

This old father reached his ripe old age. He happened to meet a monk. The monk recognized his pure service to his children. He could also see behind such enduring service there was a deep sense of attachment. The monk advised, 'You have spent several years looking after your children. Enough of attachment to your family, come and let us go to the heavenly abode — *vaikunta*, I will lead to the path to *vaikunta*.' The old man offered salutations — *pranaam*, to the monk and thanked him for his advice. He then requested the monk to give him some more time as his children were still not matured. He emphasized, '*vaikunta* will not go anywhere; but my children don't know how to manage themselves.'

After some years the old man died. The monk once again visited the nearby place and paid a visit to the old man's house. Being a wise person — *jnaani*, he could see the same old man was reborn as a cow in the same household. As the children were as irresponsible as ever, the cow was yielding more milk than usual to feed the children. The monk had a dialogue with the cow after recognizing who he was in his old birth and said, 'I know your attachment to your children. You have taken birth as a cow and now serving your children. You have done enough now, come, let us go to *Vaikunta*, let us go to heaven.' The cow pleaded, 'Give me some more time, my grandchildren are coming up, I will take good care of them. Give me little more time.' Thus the journey to paradise was lost second time even.

Attachment continues to be strong. After several years, the monk tirelessly made another visit to the household. The cow had died, and was reborn as a dog now. The monk could see through his wisdom that the dog, in its previous birth, was a cow. Earlier to that he was a father for his irresponsible children. This time as a dog, the obligation was to protect the vast number of children and grandchildren. The monk again said, 'Enough is enough, let us go to *vaikunta*, let us go to heaven. I will show you the path how to reach paradise.' The dog replied, 'My children and grandchildren are still irresponsible. Earlier, I had little less responsibility as the number was less compared to now. There are many grandchildren now and hence my responsibility is even more towards them. Please give me some more time'. Dejected and detached, the monk went away.

After some years, the monk returned yet again. He found that the dog had died and again taken another birth as a snake. It has chosen to be snake to protect all the wealth, which as an old man had stored in a corner of the garden. It is always said that if one is attached too much, one would be born as a snake. A snake was all around to protect the wealth. The monk compassionately addressed the snake and pleaded again, 'You have taken many births. Why are you so attached to your children and grandchildren who are useless in any case? At least now, leave all these and come with me. I will lead you on the path towards *vaikunta*.

The snake replied, 'No! They are still very irresponsible. They will squander all the money that I had saved for them. I did not even tell you earlier, but there is so much of wealth to protect. Let them become little more responsible. When grace of a master — *guru dasha* dawns and ill effects — *shani dasha* goes away, they will have responsibility and they can access all the wealth that I had saved for them and the wealth will thus be protected.'

The monk, out of sheer love and compassion revealed to all the people around that there is a snake in the household and departed. Sensing danger to the nearby surroundings people gathered, traced the snake, and chased it away by pounding several thrashes. Beaten black and blue the snake disappeared. People looted all the money and their joy knew no bounds at getting vast wealth… that too unexpectedly. The snake beaten, shaken and feeling hurt cried out to the monk, 'Please save me, enough is enough and let me go to *vaikunta,* the eternal paradise.'

Adi Shankaracharya says, 'Have care, but don't have attachment.' I know all of you are listening and silently saying 'this is all fine Swamiji, but in actual life you know how is this possible to practice?' I am not saying that you don't take care but you have to grow up. You have to learn to grow up. If you don't learn to grow up you get lost like the old man in the above story. *Yavad vitto parjana sakta,* so long as you are earning people are around you, then *stavannija parivaro raktah,* family also takes care of you, but once *pascha jivati jarjara dehe,* when your body becomes old, when you have no capacity to earn, most of them will wither away, unless your family has spiritual values imbibed in them. *Vartam kopi na prcchati gehe* — nobody is going to ask you about your welfare.

Therefore, what to do? So, leave your children to fend themselves and you attend discourse at a mandir. *Bhaja govindam, bhaja govindam, govindam bhaja mudhamate, samprapte sannihite kale na hi na hi raksati dukrn karane* — all this is not going to protect you. Be like a river; when a river flows through beautiful settings and sceneries, the river does not say, 'Oh, this place is pretty, let me enjoy for some more time around this scenic beauty' and get attached. No, the river just goes about its journey towards its destination.

Akaashaat patitam toyam samudram prati gachchati, water comes from the sky — *aakasha;* finally it reaches the ocean — *samudram pratigachchati.* So be like a river, go here and there, enjoy the sceneries around, do good deeds to the beautiful surroundings in your journey but remember that you have to move on and on. If you don't lead your life with this understanding and actions, you find your life would be nothing short of being miserable. Have this clarity. Once you have this understanding, as parents, you have a sense of detachment and at the same time you would shower loving and caring energy on your children. When equipped thus, you find you can genuinely contribute towards your family.

In organizations too, I have noticed there are board members or directors who are not connected to their field of competence. In one of the large companies I know, they had appointed an ex-army general as a director who had no connection to the kind of operations that the company had undertaken. When I asked a group of them as to why they appoint a person who do not possess the required expertise in their field of operation, their reply was, 'We appoint one or two board of directors who are unconnected to our field of expertise as at times we are so lost in our knowledge and perceptions with reference to the industry we are in. A person who is not well versed with our processes and field of operation would be able to provide an objective perception towards an issue that we have on hand related to well-being of the organization. Only criteria should be that one has to be an accomplished person in his field.' They even invited me to be one of their board members, as they were of the opinion that I give an objective perception even though I may be not aware of the intricacy of their business.

Therefore, I have realised that objectivity can help in contribution in the business. This objectivity in spiritual parlance is nothing but detachment.

That is why a surgeon at times finds it very difficult to

perform a surgery on his own child. He can perform a complicated surgery on someone else, but on his own child he may have apprehensions. This is because of one's identification with one's child that can be strong and in such identification the whole objectivity of a skilful surgery may not have the desired result.

Therefore, please understand that if you are a parent full of attachments to name, fame and power and advise your children to be good mannered, profess nobler values and try to guide them in many ways that you as a parent feel appropriate, the result would be something like this — your advise would be like hot potatoes that are being dropped.

A family went on a holiday to Hawaiian beach. The child asked his mother if he could enjoy playing in the sands of the beautiful beach. The mother said, 'No dear, don't play in the sand, you will dirty your hands.' After sometime the child asked if he could enjoy playing with those inviting waves of the ocean. The mother again retarded, 'No, you already have a throat infection. It would only worsen.' The child persisted, 'Can I atleast join other kids who are playing on the road?' The mother said, 'No, please don't do that. There are vehicles plying all around. And you have a tendency to get lost.' The child started crying. The mother shared with other holiday makers, 'I don't understand my child. In spite of undertaking an expensive holiday in Hawaii, he is crying.'

Tell me who is the problem now; is it the child or the parents? Now she is praying to God, *Bhaja Govindam*. 'Oh!

Lord, in spite of making it for a holiday and that too in scenic Hawaii, my child is crying', actually the bigger problem lies with the parent.

Andrew Carnegie, one time among the richest man in the world was asked in an interview, 'Sir, you have earned enough. You could have easily retired at any point of time of your choice.' He said, 'I do not know how to stop earning the money. I know only how to earn money. I know only this... one track of earning money. I do not know how to stop earning money.'

I tell you this is very meaningful and one can profit learning a lesson from it. Some people do not know how and when to stop. Even at the ripe age of over ninety years, people are still thinking of making money, money and more money. How and when to stop earning money is also very important aspect of life... and therefore, please feel this example.

Adi Shankaracharya says enough of attachment to worldly affairs. Enough of attachment to near and dear ones, but have a caring energy. With such a caring energy if one starts working in the world, one can genuinely contribute in whatever field of activity one is engaged in. Ultimately, if we were to look closely, our attachments are giving attention to something. We are attached means we are giving attention more than required. We know how to give *undue* attention to objects, persons and other things in the world outside but we do not know how to give *required* attention to the feelings and emotions to our inner world.

We are attached to non-essentials but we seldom provide attention to the essentials in life.

The way you direct your attention is the way you direct your life. So don't be upset against your undue attachments. It is an indicator of where your attachment is leading to. Once you understand where your attachment is leading to, gently ask a question to yourself, 'Is this a wise approach? If the answer is no, then what do you do next? Slowly steer such attachments towards the inner. *Bhaja Govindam Bhaja Govindam Govindam Bhaja Mudhamate*. It is like how a mother goes about coaxing a child tirelessly, one has to coax one's mind lovingly... enough of living on primitive pleasures like sucking the thumb. Turn towards the Lord, turn to seek the higher, be in the macro and do not get lost in the micro is the direction one has to be placed in. Thus, *Bhaja Govindam Bhaja Govindam Govindam Bhaja Mudhamate*. Have you understood only from your head oriented understanding or from heart oriented feelings?

Please close your eyes. I want you to feel the verse. Feel it with love. Keep your eyes closed. When your intellect comprehends this understanding it is beautiful but also make effort to feel from your heart oriented centre. This would be wonderful.

Yavadvittoparjanasakta
Stavannijaparivaro Raktah
Pascajjivati Jarjaradehe
Vartam Kopi Na Prchhati gehe

Bhaja govindam bhaja govindam,
Govindam bhaja mudhamate,
Samprapte sannihite kale,
Na hi na hi raksati dukrn karane.

Pray! Let this prayer emerge from your heart. Seek the Divine; learn to invoke the blessings of the Divine. Learn to pray, 'Oh! Lord, enough of this childish play, Oh! Lord, endow me with higher tastes to flower forth into a potential that you have blessed me with. How long am I going to log on to the primitive game of running after my own shadow?' Learn to stop and seek the Lord, seek the Lord and seek the Lord.

Continuing further.

VERSE 6

The essence behind the wonderful instrument called the body

यावत्पवनो निवसति देहे
तावत्पृच्छति कुशलं गेहे ।
गतवति वायौ देहापाये
भार्या बिभ्यति तस्मिन्काये ।।
(भज-गोविन्दं... भज-गोविन्दं) (१)

Yavatpavano Nivasati Dehe
Tavatprcchati Kusalam gehe
Gatavati Vayau Dehapaye
Bharya Bibhyati Tasminkaye
(Bhaja-Govindam Bhaja-Govindam...) (6)

यावत् – as long as, पवन: – the breath, निवसति – resides, देहे – in (your) body, तावत् – so long, पृच्छति – enquires, कुशलं – of (your) well-being, गेहे – at home, गतवति, वायौ – when the breath leaves, देह अपाये – (when) the body decays, भार्या – (even) your wife, बिभ्यति – fears, तस्मिन् – that very (in that very), काये – body, भज – Seek, गोविन्दं – Govinda

As long as there resides breath in the body, so long they enquire of your well-being at home. Once the breath leaves, the body decays, even your wife fears that very same body. (Seek Govinda, seek Govinda).

Yavatpavano nivasati dehe tavat prcchati kusalam gehe – so long as there is breath in your life, so long as there is breath air flowing through your nostrils, Adi Shankaracharya continues further... Please feel the verses and listen by using both your heart centre and an open mind.

So long as there is life breath circulating in your body, well-wishers are going to enquire about your well-being — *kusalam*, they will ask how are you? — *kusalam va samichanam va.* But the moment the breath goes — *gatavati vaayav deha paaye,* – wife or husband will get scared of you — *bharyaa bibhyati tasmin kaaye.* As we learnt before, a husband or wife not just loves one's body but the very life that runs through in and out of the body — *praana.*

Are we focused on *praana shakti*, or are we just focused on physical self? Constantly we nurture, decorate and pamper the body alone without much of attention being paid to the inner self. The very essence of one's life is the *praana shakti.*

How many of us spend time and energy at looking a little deeper than just attending to the needs of one's body? There is something more beyond one's body. The body exists in some locus. So the master says, *'Yavatpavano nivasati dehe tavat prcchati kusalam gehe gatavati vayau dehapaye bharya bibhyati tasminkaye.'*

Should one get angry with one's wife or husband? No. Just understand that one is beyond the comprehension of the body. There is something more in a husband or a wife than just the manifestation of a body. This is a fact. Do not lose sight of this vital truth.

Adi Shankaracharya wants us to re-program our whole perception of ourselves. In the *Bhagavad Gita*, the Lord beautifully says, 'This body is only like a dress — *vaasaamsi jeernaani yatha vihaaya navaani grihnnaati naroparaani*. Just because one's body is like a dress, it does not mean that one has to handle it badly. But if one understands the very dress to be oneself, it is a great foolishness.

So let us develop wisdom that the dress is not the real 'we'. It is like saying, 'I am not the dress and the dress is mine, so also the body is mine but I am not the body'. The master wants us to think little more deeply. Superficially, we all have thoughts but let us take a deeper look into it.

For example, say your name is Prem Sagar. The purpose of giving you such name by your parents is that you have to be like an ocean of love. Superficially, you are knowing that you are known as Prem Sagar is not good enough. You have to live your life true to your name. You should experience the meaning of the name and your being should reflect that you are an ocean of Love.

Take the case of my name. Swami Sukhabodhananda — *sukhena bodhayati ca asau anandaha* — the one who teaches joyously and blissfully.

Please understand this very clearly. Krishna, Buddha, Mahavira, Christ are not just ordinary persons; they are more than their names which rings an inspirational awe in us. They were not mere philosophers. They were more than the philosophers. They were and are the presence.

Krishna is a presence. Buddha is a presence. Mahavira is a presence. We have to savour the presence, but what do we do? We worship their form but we forget the essentials that they are the presence. So that presence we have to invite — *avahanam*, to that presence we surrender — *avahanam samarpayami*. If we are truly worshipping Lord Krishna, we should be playful like Lord Krishna, have the qualities like *ananda lahari, prema lahari* and *soundarya lahari* but not take life very seriously.

Let us lead life in a space of lightness and at the same time have flexibility to be intense in what we undertake to do. Lord Krishna is a representation of a multi-dimensional energy. So if one is a Krishna *bhakta*, one has to bring forth such energies in all activities.

Buddha represents silence and highly compassionate. So they are all a state of presence, and let us not forget their core essence which is indeed their presence.

You would be doing a great favour to your parents if you live your life to the meaning of your name. In this context please understand that the body is like a dress. Respect the dress, care for your body. If you genuinely care for your body, I wonder you would ever abuse the body. If you care for someone, you do not harm such person. Isn't it? If you care for your body, you won't harm the body. If you don't harm the body, you will do what is appropriate for the welfare of the body.

Adi Shankaracharya wants us to bring forth the caring energy. Once you start caring, you are focused in giving right attention. Once you are giving attention, you come in touch with the fact that the body is alive due to life force within — *praana shakti*. When *praana shakti* leaves one is said to be dead. So can a beloved say that he or she is in love with one's *praana shakti*? There is a substratum — *adishtaanam*, in which the *praana shakti* exists. What is that substratum? The substratum is the very self — *atma*.

Therefore, the Vedas declare, '*atmanastu kamaya sarvam priyam bhavati*'. Ultimately, we all love the atma. All these understanding are based on the reflection that leads one to one's own true self — the *atma shakti*. Unfortunately, we fall in love with the shadow like a dress and forget the person — the *atma*. Please get this distinction very clearly.

So make an attempt to bring in caring energy in whatever you undertake. In this context reflect on the verse, *yavat pavano nivasati dehe* – so long as there is the life energy — *praana shakti*, the body has luster and others hanker after it and enquire about its welfare. When the *praana shakti* leaves nobody bothers. *Praana shakti* — breath represents life.

What is life? Please think deeply. Slowly you start realizing that it is nothing other than the God principle, isn't it? Can God be other than life? No, God cannot be other than life. If God is other than life, God is lifeless. Thus God cannot be other than life. God is life. Life is God. And when you start caring for life, you are caring for God and caring for God is caring for life. The caring makes you connect, really imbibe the energy, and therefore the very life itself is God.

Thus, *Bhajagovindam, bhaja govindam govindam bhaja mudhamate*. Oh, Fool! The master goes on addressing.

When he addresses you as a fool and provokes you, you start thinking. At least some awakening happens in your intellect or else you will be in deep slumber like *Kumbhakarna,* a character from *Ramayana* who used to sleep half the year. Many births you have been squandering in slumber; most of the present life is spent on the non-essential, therefore, please internalise this understanding. If you lead a life with this understanding life becomes extremely beautiful.

Yavat pavano nivasati dehe tavat prcchati kusalam gehe. Gatavati vayau deha paye. I am constantly repeating this verse because it should be like a lullaby in your life. The whole understanding has to be nicely churned and digrested into one's system. *Gatavati vayau deha paye,* when *praana shakti* goes away even your spouse will not be able to enquire your well-being. Your spouse may also have similar question because she/he is a representation of life similar to above understanding. Between these two lives... that is yourself and your spouse, if you think you both are different, it is only because you have not learnt how to view life with churning and understanding as unfolded above.

As I told you, we know how to read printed books or words, but we do not know how to comprehend the language of unprinted words like one's presence. We are not able to see the deeper significance of sunrise, the deeper significance of nature's bounty. The moment we are able to comprehend the significance of them, a non-verbal communication, a formless communication happens within us and we find a different type of awakening happens in us.

Thus, you are an expression of life and your spouse is also an expression of life. Please enquire what is life all about? When you do start enquiring thus, you will see for example, the great philosophy called *ghataakaasha* and *mahaakasha*.

It can be explained like this. There is a *ghata* — a pot and there is *akaasha* — space in a pot. There is space in a pot and assume that a pot is placed in this hall, hall space is something much bigger than a pot space. Now the pot space feels very inferior because of the hall space being much bigger than the pot space. Thus, the pot space feels inferior to the hall space in this case. The master is asking us to enquire, 'Find out who is in the space'.

It is like he is asking us to find out what is life on the similar line of finding out who is in the space. If you take close look at this space, the obvious question would be — does the space exist in the pot or the pot exists in the space? *Varam varam* — yet again and again constantly think! Does the space exist in the pot or the pot exists in the space? For example, if you say space exists in the pot, the master says please change your paradigm of seeing. If you were to see closely and observe in detail, you see the pot in fact exists in this space. The space does not exist in the pot; but the pot exists in space.

So, the key is to change your perception. When you change the perception you have to say the pot exists in space, because without this space where can a pot exist? In such a scenario of understanding the space in the pot will not feel limited to a pot, because the space in the pot is not limited by the pot. When you look at the space from the angle of space, you comprehend undoubtedly, the pot exists in space.

Similarly, the body is like a pot, isn't it? The body is like a pot. There is something called as *chidambaram chaitanya* in this body.

There are life principles governing the body. If one were to look from the angle of the body, consciousness is limited to the body. Therefore, when the body dies it appears as though that the consciousness has left the body. It is similar to when a pot is broken, it appears that pot space is also taken away but the fact is that — only a pot is broken. But if one looks from an angle of 'pot space is taken away', but is really space gone? No. A pot space has not gone anywhere but a pot is broken. In effect a pot space got merged in the total space. Subtly seen, there is no merging. Only a pot space collapses and disappears.

Similarly, when the body dies, it appears that the soul or *atma* has gone. No it is not true. That feeling occurs when you are looking from the angle of the body. From the angle of space, the body is like a wave in the ocean of consciousness — *taranga*. It arises, exists, and disappears into consciousness like the wave rises, exists and disappears into an ocean.

Avyaktani bhutani vyaktamakyana bharata avyakta nivananeva patraka pariverana – from the unmanifest *avyaktani bhudani vyaktmatyani bharata* – come the manifest and goes back to the unmanifest. The waves come from an ocean, exist in an ocean and merges back into an ocean. Even the birth and death of waves in an ocean are just an illusion.

Similarly, when the body is destroyed it does not mean the self — *atma* has gone away. No! When a pot is destroyed, it appears as though the space is destroyed. If one starts seeing from the angle of space, one understands that when a pot is destroyed, pot space is not destroyed.

Thus, if one sees from the angle of body, when the body dies it appears as though the self — *atma* is gone away. But seen from the angle of the self — *atma*, when the body dies, the self — *atma* does not go away. Therefore, Adi Shankaracharya is focusing our attention to look within, look at our lives. But most of us are trained to look outside. When we start looking within, we come in touch with a reality that neither death unduly upset us nor birth results in over joy. Both the phenomenon are like roles as far as the body is concerned.

Reflect on this story that I recently read.

A student asked a master as to why he was not condemning the rich people enough. The Master asked why should he criticise someone unnecessarily. The student retarded, 'Poor people understand spiritual concepts easily. There is a strong feeling that being rich and practice of spirituality do not go hand in hand. If one is more inclined to spirituality, one has to be necessarily poor.'

The Master said, 'Look at a shadow of a bamboo tree. It does not affect a garden. When a bamboo tree sways to the gentle breeze the shadow of the bamboo tree sweeps the garden. But the shadow of the bamboo tree does not affect the garden in any way, right? Similarly, when an understanding dawns, neither wealth nor poverty affects such a person.'

Why am I saying this? There is a strong case for our perception to change. Therefore, the great *guru* constantly invites us to look within. Look within and see clearly this fact — so long as life breath exists in one, one's body is alive. Life breath when goes away makes the body dead. Look at what life breath is. Take care of the body. The body is alive, because of the life breath. Even a dog understands who master of the house is. Unfortunately, we do not seem to know who our master is. What a plight has become of us?

I have seen some people worshipping their body. Look! The body is alive because of life breath or *praana*. *Praana* exists because of space – the self or *atma*; who do we love? *Atmanastu kamaya sarvam priyam bhavati* – our love is truly directed towards the *atma*. Therefore, the *atma* is one's life, one's spouse's life. God cannot be lifeless. Life and God are synonyms and since both are synonyms – *Bhaja govindam, bhaja govindam, govindam bhaja mudhamate*. Still if understanding does not get inside deeply, what do we do? If such teaching cannot shake one up, then leave it to nature. It has its own methods to shake up one from deep slumber.

Varam varam, constantly think — a great discerning in oneself and awakening will happen. I have said this very often but still I repeat – some seeds were discovered in the

Egyptian Pyramid, it is said they were more than a thousand years old. There was an experiment carried wherein those seeds were planted again. Surprisingly, the seeds started sprouting. When I read this incident it did touch me deeply.

We are like pyramids of the bygone era. Due to some acquired good fortune — *punya,* our *gurus* and *rishis* have thrown some seeds at us. Don't think it is a waste. These seeds are present in us in a primitive form, seeds of teaching are present in some form, but all of a sudden when the seeds of understanding are sown in a fertile space of openness and learning, the seeds are bound to sprout. Just trust this.

Therefore, even if one does not understand what Adi Shankaracharya is trying to convey lovingly, it does not matter to oneself at this point of time. With devotion — *bhakti,* and faith — *shraddha* if one were to listen as the seeds are scattered in oneself, sprouts are bound to grow. Due to some *punya* one is listening, bereft of it, it is not possible.

As one is listening from pure heart filled with devotion and faith, the third force called grace will descend and one finds seeds of understanding start sprouting. Therefore, ultimately everything is a product of grace, but one has to prepare oneself in the right path for grace to descend.

I was reading the great Ramana Maharishi's work. He unfolds that one can push one's effort up to a certain point and after that nothing remains in one's hand. A grace like a gentle breeze will sweep across one's being. Enlightenment happens just like a breeze, one has no control over it.

My *guru* used to say you should have patience for a thousand years to remain quiet but keep your effort in preparing. The grace will happen in its own course of time. But the process of preparation is an important aspect of one's living. So, constantly spend lifetime in reflecting and preparation. It may not click in you immediately, but carry on reflecting and who knows suddenly some clicking may happen. It can happen in a most uncertain way. Say for example, you may be watching a movie and an understanding can come about through the movie. When an understanding dawns, you may not know.

The great saint Vemana from Andhra was so attached to his body and one day his wife asked him a question, 'You have so much of love towards your body, but if you start loving the soul what would happen?' It triggered something profound in him and he went on to become one of the greatest saints. Therefore, you have to prepare yourself and leave the rest in the hands of the Almighty. No hurry, no expectation. I am emphasizing as in some of you a new tension would arise — enlightenment tension or God realization tension or some will say, 'I have to realise God, Swamiji.' It results in more tension.

You should be like both a *markata*, where a baby monkey hold on to the mother monkey and also should be like a *bidala*, cat where mother cat picks up its kitten. This is an act of surrender. You put in your best efforts like a baby monkey and also leave it in the care of the Divine like a kitten to its mother. Thereafter, it is the factor called grace that will simply take charge of you.

Reflect on this Zen story.

☙A lady was carrying a pot filled with water. The pot fell down. When the pot fell down, it is said, she became enlightened. She wrote the book called, 'No Moon, No Water'. Taking a clue from this story many people just aped her and went about breaking the pots. But nothing happened…only their money, energy and time was wasted.

Breaking the pot was not important, it was only incidental. The lady in the story was so well prepared that grace dawned and swept her away.

The poet Lakshmidhara kavi says,

> *Kataaksha kiranachaanta*
> *namanmohabdaye namaha*
> *anantaanand krishnaaya*
> *jagan mangala murtaye.*

The above verse denotes – Oh! Master, please do not look at me so directly; I don't want that much of your grace. The rays of your sideward glance is more than enough — *Kataaksha kirana*, to burn away — *aachanta*, the ocean of ignorance — *mohabdaye namaha*, Why? You are limitless and your presence is auspiciousness — *Anantaananda Krishnaaya jaganmangalamoortaye*, the whole world — *jagat*, is auspicious. It is with *devotion* — *bhakti*, and wisdom — *gnana*, when grace falls — *anugraha*, the blind can see and the lame can walk — *mookam karoti vachaalam pangum langayate girim.*

Why am I quoting this verse? It is to remind you that apart from one's wife's or husband's tension or financial tension or work tension or social tension... a new tension called God tension should not envelop you. A new enlightenment tension should not engulf you. You are all laughing when I say this but in reality I do see people who come and tell me that the only tension for them is enlightenment tension. But what does enlightenment mean? As long as 'I' is present in one, one is far way from the state of enlightenment. The 'I' should disappear, dissolve and cut off from the deep layer or core of one's being.

Hence, please make sincere effort for the 'I' to disappear, dissolve and root out from your system. The moment you make sincere effort, somewhere fruits of action — *karma siddhi,* would bear its results in the form of grace. It is some mysterious happening; there is an effort that one makes and it follows with effortless understanding. That is the contradiction *of siddhi,* effort. You make all the effort, but the understanding comes about effortlessly. Constantly reflect over. So,

Bhaja govindam, bhaja govindam,
govindam bhaja mudhamate.
Samprapte sannihite kale
na hi na hi raksati dukrn karane.

Please close your eyes and feel from your heart; from your head oriented understanding you have heard enough from me. Now, I want you to understand from you heart. Close your eyes, connect to your heart, and try to understand this verse from your heart.

Yavatpavano Nivasati Dehe
Tavatprcchati Kusalam gehe
Gatavati Vayau Dehapaye
Bharya Bibhyati Tasminkaye
(Bhaja-Govindam Bhaja-Govindam...)

Literally pray for the Divine. 'Oh! Lord, give me the understanding that which is purely your grace, Oh! Lord.' Learn to cry out for infinite; learn to yearn like a small child. 'Oh! Lord, bless me an understanding to dispel the ocean of ignorance, in which I am not fully drowned as yet, but surely drowning.'

The Lord provides us with a map... the map of how our lives should shape up. Sometimes, it could also be the map of failure that in turn supports us to be successful. Not only the map of success that help us to be successful but the map of failure also will help us to be successful, so that we don't repeat a mistake.

Take a close look at the map of some people, on how their lifetime is spent. In a very poetic simple nutshell a conclusion can be made in a grape fruit style — *draakshi phalam* filled with poetry from the heart, and the sharpness of the head and the enlightened words of Adi Shankaracharya.

VERSE 7

Four pillars for wise living to reach the ultimate

बालस्तावत्क्रीडासक्तः
तरुणस्तावत्तरुणीसक्तः ।
वृद्धस्तावच्चिन्तासक्तः
परमे ब्रह्मणि कोऽपि न सक्तः ॥
(भज-गोविन्दं... भज-गोविन्दं) (७)

Balastavatkridasaktah
Tarunastavattarunisaktah
Vrddhastavaccintasaktah
Parame Brahmani Kopi Na Saktah
(Bhaja-Govindam Bhaja-Govindam...) (7)

बालः तावत् – so long as one is in one's childhood, क्रीडा – (towards play) to play, आसक्तः – (one is) attached, तरुणः तावत् – a youth (so long as one is in youth), तरुणी – towards young women (towards passion), सक्तः – (one is) attached, वृद्धः तावत् – so long as one is old (an old man), चिन्ता – towards anxiety, आसक्तः – (one is) attached, परमे – to the supreme, ब्रह्मणि – Brahman, कः अपि – any one (alas), न – no, सक्तः – attached, भज – Seek, गोविन्दं – Govinda

During childhood one is attached to play, during youth one is attached to women. In old age one is attached to anxiety... yet, no one is attached to supreme Brahman. (Seek Govinda, seek Govinda).

Please see that your life does not end up like a catastrophe. He says, when you are a small child — *balastavat krida saktah,* you are lost in play — *krida.* A child lost in play is understandable, but having grown up, your childishness continues. Adi Shankaracharya says 'understandably, as a child you are lost in play', but the word '*aasaktaha*', attached to play, it is 'the attachment' that he is emphasizing for us to dwell deep. He questions, 'Have people really grown up?' Throughout, I have been saying that we don't grow up but we only grow old. There is only ageing that is happening for sure. There is no growth that is really taking place.

So he says, 'When you are a child, you are attached to play. It is understandable. But as you grow up this attachment continues, yet the play may not continue — the *baalavastha,* may not continue, but the attachment continues. When you are born to youth, you are stuck, attached, lost, infatuated, addicted, blown or carried away by the opposite sex — *tarunastavattaruni saktah.*

At childhood there was one type of addiction, at youth there is yet other type of addiction. Now look when you become old, there remains only worry and worry — *vrddhastavaccintasaktah,* because having led a life where as a child enjoying playing and as a youth in the interest of opposite sex. That is why chain of worries haunts during old age — *vrddhastavaccintasaktah.*

What is Truth? — *Parame brahmani kopi na saktah* — What is enlightenment? Is there such a thing called Nirvana? Is there really Moksha or it is just a concept.

No such questions are enquired into at all during the prime time of one's life. The whole life time is spent on eating like *Bakaasura*, sleeping like *Kumbhakarana* and living like *Ravana*.

The above three characters represent three lowly form of existence of characters represented in the texts of *Mahabharata* and *Ramayana* respectively. And then you expect your life to be like a garden filled with flowers. It does not happen that way. As it does not happen the way you wish to happen, your whole life becomes miserable. Therefore, the master asks us to please tackle the very base of one's attachment.

Now I want you to understand very clearly. As a child you are lost in play. This is understandable, but the childishness continues upon one's growing years. But if you continue the 'child-likeness', there is maturity, but if you continue this 'childishness', there is no maturity, and you are lost. You can be with member of opposite sex, *taruni* but with child-like innocence.

Have you seen in some youth — when their love is not reciprocated or spurned by their beloved, laila, or majnu, what they resort to? Cheap thrills like pouring acid and disfiguring the face of the person they love...thus leaving a deep scar in the very life of someone who once was desirable. One is totally lost and turns into being inhuman. If one is after attraction to opposite sex, *taruni,* there is no problem in that.

In fact, it is indeed natural. But when it leads into the domain of stupidity there is a grave danger. It is this childishness or stupidity that we have to transform. Between being 'childishness', and 'child-likeness', there is very big difference — a *childlikeness* is innocent like a child while *childishness* is ignorant like a child.

Therefore, when one is enlightened and posses a quality of being childlike, in such a space one start responding to various aspects of one's life. For me true childlikeness is responding to life, childishness is reacting to life. One has to make a decision whether one is responding to life situations or reacting to life situations.

If one were to change the programming of one's mindset that one's being has to be like childlike, there emerges a quality of innocence which invites one to, 'Yes, in life we have to respond to life situations.' When one ultimately reaches an enlightened state, one would be like a dry leaf. One would be able to flow with the breeze of life and be ready to receive the grace of the Divine.

Please close your eyes. Let us all chant Om. Being inwardly silent and in a still mind learn to seek the Divine and His blessings. Just feel as though your mother's caring hands are placed on your head and take her blessings — *maatru devo bhava*. Feel as though your father's loving hands are placed on your head and take his blessings — *pitru devo bhava*. Similarly feel as though your *guru's* hands are placed on your head and take his blessings – *acharya devo bhava*. Let us pray to this great saint Adi Shankaracharya to bless us with a deeper meaning of the verses of *Bhaja Govindam* and fill our hearts.

Balastavatkridasaktah

Tarunastavattarunisaktah

Vrddhastavaccintasaktah

Parame Brahmani Kopi Na Saktah

(Bhaja-Govindam Bhaja-Govindam...)

I want you to realise this wonderful silence within.

You have been seeing the life map, which generally attracts one to living a life of deficiency — *samsaara*. The Upanishads offer us two paths — the path of *shreyas* and the path of *preyas*. The path of *preyas* is the path of deficiency — *samsara*, and the path of *shreyas* is the path of inner freedom — *nirvana*. Now you have to make a choice. Do you want the path of deficiency or the path of inner freedom?

The word *nirvana* — inner freedom is beautiful. In Sanskrit *nirvana* means blowing off. *Nirvana* means blowing off one's petty ego, one's little candle or one's acquisitions. The path of *preyas* means enlightenment or *moksha* and this is the essence or the ultimate goal of one's life.

Nirvana is the essence. Please understand this. *Nirvana* is the essence — *taatparya*. *Nirvana* means blowing off. Blowing off what? It is one's ego. Why should one blow one's ego? Because the ego feels that it is in conflict with the macro. The micro feels it is in conflict with the macro. When micro feels in conflict with macro, one is bound to live a dis-harmonious life.

'Ahankaara vimoodhaatma karta iti manyate.' The Lord says, 'The one who leads a life filled with ego is not just a fool,

but he is a great fool indeed.' So if one is choosing a path of ultimate good — *shreyas*, one should work on blowing off and let go of the little candle called ego. Once the little candle called ego is blown off, the new blue print of life opens its fold.

The life led as per the new blue print leads one to the path of ultimate good — *shreyas*. In the path of *shreyas*, like how step by step one goes about building a structure... architect, plan and detailing are essential among many other essentials for converting the objective into a reality. Our *rishis* have discovered the path of ultimate good — *shreyas*, and the blue print is the path of enlightenment — *nirvana* or *moksha*.

What should be the steps that one has to undertake? The steps prescribed in the scriptures are — the states of *brahmacharya, grihasta, vaanaprastha and sanyaasa*. This is the track laid since several centuries in the Indian culture.

Let us take them one by one. The stage of bachelorhood — *brahmacharya avastha*, is a stage wherein one devotes most of one's time and energy in study, contemplation and self remembering. Study involves gathering knowledge of not only about the world but also about one's multiple dimension of life and its relations. So, *swaadhyaayam na pramatitavyam* — the Veda says.

Don't stop studying about one-self — *swaadhyaayam*. So in the state of bachelorhood — *brahmachyarya*, one is engrossed in study of self, study of the scriptures and constantly observing oneself. One can observe oneself only in contrast with one's relationship with others.

Therefore, one says, 'I am observing myself, observing the world, observing the connection between me and the world.'

And in the whole observation finds out the way to blow off the inner candle called ego. The ways and means that are involved to finally blow off one's ego is the ultimate lesson for realisation.

This is not a simple task. It is indeed a great task spread over one's lifetime or may be even more. If the map explained as above is clearly understood, in the stage of bachelorhood — *brahmacharya avastha*, and in the *gurukulam* — ancient name for a boarding school, one studies this profound understanding — *vidya*. The result may not accrue overnight. Through dedication one studies and after completion of study how does one goes about thereafter?

For example, you pass out of engineering with distinction; it does not mean to say you are a great engineer. The reality is that you are equipped to go and start working. Your working experience will deepen your academic study. On the similar lines, during *brahmacharya avastha* the blue print of the *rishis* is given to a seeker to study. Thus, having studied, the field would then be open for the seeker to deal with the world outside and prepares himself to embrace the next step. That is the life of a householder — grahasthaashrama.

Therefore, it can be easily said that the passport for marriage is the life of householder — *grihasthashram*. For example, a doctor studying in the field of medicine cannot perform a surgery. What would be the result of such adventurism? Just imagine a person saying — don't worry I am a very intelligent person, and I am studying all aspects of medicine and I can perform the surgery. If he does so, the operation would be successful but the patient would collapse, isn't it?

What is happening right now in our lives is something like this. Marriage means only getting progeny... why even buffaloes also produce their off-springs, cockroaches also produce their off-springs hence why not anyone? That is why most of the marriages are in such a mess around us.

In ancient times, during the life of *Gurukulam*, one would focus on the study of the self — *swaadhyaayanam* means *swasya adhyayanam* — study of the self. One is observing and studying oneself deeply into the realms of what is this mind, what are its conflict, where does it emerges from, what is the purpose of very life and such details. One studies all these aspects thoroughly even if one is an average student.

It is more out of adherence to discipline of a well laid out system by a *guru*. The state and the regime of *Brahmacharya* or the stage of bachelorhood prepares one to embrace the life of a householder or *grihastha*. Thereafter, one would necessarily put the learnings of *gurukulam* into practise. What is the essence of all this — *taatparya*?

Nirvana! Nirvana means blowing off the inner candle of ego. But, if this simple shift is not practised one is bound to develop an ego in married life also. Have you observed that many parents are angry with their children because children are not following what they say? Not following what they are saying means they want their ego to be endorsed.

Yet I have come across many who say, 'I love my children.' More than loving our children, I feel one is loving one's opinion of their children. If a son gets married to a girl belonging to another community, he is banished from all family ties. They fail to understand that he has after all married a human being only and not a buffalo or a cockroach; but banishing from the family is the result.

Please come in touch with this reality as to who you are really loving? But you return to me by justifying, 'Swamiji, don't I have the freedom to tell my children who they have to marry?'

Do you think your son is like a pet or a sacrificial animal that he should just follow you? Your son may counter, 'Let me decide my suffering, why should parents decide with whom I should suffer with?' Most of the parents get upset to this reality.

I am telling you honestly. Truth is bitter, lot of parents do get upset, all because they are not following what I am saying. They would want their choice and their 'I' to dominate the life of their children. In the role of discharging the responsibilities of a house holder, *grihasthashram,* their ego is more cemented.

When the ego becomes stronger and stronger, and thus one leads life predominantly directed by the pull of great deceiver called ego, the arrival of old age appears somewhat sudden, unwelcome, and distasteful. But that is a reality one cannot do anything about than to just embrace in totality.

During old age the life gets much murkier and messier. The great saint Adi Shankaracharya says, 'vrddhastavaccintasaktah — when one becomes old — vrddha, most go about worrying. That is the path of the life of deficiency — samsara. But why is it so? Because as one lives a life full of ignorance, there exists ego which is both visible and invisible, but highly destructive in its very nature.

Some people have more egos, some fewer egos, and some may be in moderation. All categories are present, but whatever it is, the ego is in the store-house of an individual. Many would have cheated you in your lifetime; many would have upset you over the years. Why should life become a mess in old age? People have cheated you, upset you, and as you grow old, if you have not adopted the path of ultimate good – shreyas, all through your life, all that you have undergone shows up as bitter taste.

Because of this, there are chances that you enter into a shell. You don't want to mix freely with people. You want to be choosy, cautious about the company that you want to keep and spend time with. You conclude that being cautious and being careful is a good virtue. It is definitely a good thing, but at times being over cautious itself can be a trap. Because many people have cheated on you, you become cautious about whom you mix with. It is like a bird captivated in a cage. No doubt the cage provides security to a bird, but the cage is in fact, a life curtailing trap to a bird.

Similarly, when old people's lives turn out in a mess, they try to be very cautious and this very cautiousness and extra carefulness by itself becomes like a death before they actually die.

The adventure of fluidity disappears in their lives, the child-likeness quality vanishes and suspicion increases in their very thinking process. They start doubting people around as they have experienced series of mishaps of having many people cheating on them. Therefore, the master places emphasis on *vrddhastavaccintasaktah,* when old age strikes, one is lost in worry, worries and more worry.

Life led on the path of ultimate good — *shreyas,* the path of enlightenment — *moksha,* results in the essence — *taatpariya* called elimination of ego — *nirvana.* Life of bachelorhood — *brahmacharya* prepares the ground like studying pure science while the life of house holder — *grihastha* is a field of experiences. As a husband or wife, whenever there is difference, I suggest that you reflect on what you have studied during the years of *gurukulam.* If you have learnt that whenever differences crop up learn to operate and be above differences.

This in turn gives you a chance to work on the core of differences. But if you don't have the essential meaning — *taatparya,* you are on the path of a life of deficiency — *samsara,* that compels you to brand differences as equal to life is empty and meaningless.

If you have studied in the *brahmacharya avastha,* as a student you are well versed in the process of teaching in the *gurukulam* system, you appreciate what Krishna in the

Bhagavad Gita emphasised and you imbibe the central message of the *vedas*. It is said, '*Siddhihi asuttayohu...*' What does it mean?

In success and failure, have the equal state of calm and serene mind – *samabhaavana*. In joy — *sukha* and sorrow — *dukha*, be in a state of *samabhaavana*. Victory — *jaya* and failure — *ajaya*, treat both with *samabhaavana*. Success and failure, demonstrate the virtues of *samabhavana*.

Such a person develops a spiritual will to be calm and serene — *sama*, and open. Bereft of this understanding whenever differences crop up, one may be inclined to say — 'My differences are defined when my spouse nods yes to my needs or when my spouse endorses me. So my happiness is dependent on somebody's yes and somebody's no. Therefore my happiness is entrapped in the situation — *sandarbh.*'

But the *Rishis, Yogis* and the *Siddhas* have repeatedly in many words have declared — happiness is neither dependent on success nor on failure. If we can understand their teachings and lead life thus, our whole blessed life changes significantly. This is a great secret. The programming of a *samsari* — a person on the path of worldly knowledge — *preyas,* is that when any desires are fulfilled he/she is happy, when somebody endorses one feels elated.

When somebody does not endorse or recognizes, he/she is miserable. Unfortunately, this is a basic structure of a programming dependent upon the other not independent — *paratantram natu swatantram.*

Suppose, while I am giving a talk, if my talk were to depend upon your smile, or your endorsement, or upon your creed, or caste, or position in the society, my happiness is dependent and it is entrapped by you. In such a scenario, I tend to become dependent — *paratantram.* Where is my freedom — *swatantram?*

Stretching the example further, you as my student having studied and attempt your hand in addressing a gathering and someone may not appreciate your talk. When you are not appreciated, your lower mind may think, 'I am not happy because somebody is not appreciating me', but then your higher mind will come into picture and counter that thinking by questioning, 'What did I study and what is my *Swadhyaayam?*'

In fact, it is one of the disciplines where a monkhood — *sanyasi,* after taking up the life of renunciation — *sanyas* is supposed to wander. In the process, he may encounter many situations wherein someone may praise him, to which he should guard against not getting blown off, and when someone criticises him, he should not feel shattered.

Having taken the life style of a *sanyasi,* he has to practice what he has learnt and appraise himself of the essence of the teachings that happiness is neither dependent upon success nor failure. What a great liberation lie in such a life led with this understanding.

This is the path of ultimate good — *shreyas.* When a husband and wife differences exist, work on differences, but never equate happiness should be dependent on the spouse. However, by force of habit one may feel it is dependent on the spouse. No problem. Supposing if your teeth are unclean what do you do? You brush them thoroughly.

Similarly, so your mind at time becomes foggy, cluttered and unclear. This happens especially when someone does not endorse your views or when you are unhappy. The remedy is to look and work on cleansing your mind repeatedly — *manasi vicintaya varam varam*, with the understanding of the verse, '*Bhaja govindam, bhaja govindam, govindam bhaja mudhamate.*' Thus it would help you in cleansing the mind again and yet again. Slowly this understanding would spread to your being and over a period of time its result would show up in your actions.

The role of a house holder *or Grihastha ashram* is a field something similar to the field of applied science. The learnings have to be applied in all walks of one's life. If applied sincerely, it can result in a wonderful field — *kseshtra*, for us to practice. *Sanyasis* like me are supposed to wander. People praise, people criticise, some even say why do I wear a watch? I just wearing a watch become an issue or topic of their discussion.

When I counsel on the issues like family and relationship, instead of focussing on the issues related to their well-being they conclude that *sadhus* never understand their problems. Either way, when we receive praise or when we receive criticism, we have to say to ourselves that our happiness is not depending on people's view or judgement of us. Happiness is *antah sukham*. *Sukham*, happiness is *antah*, within you.

So, as a *sanyasi* this approach by itself is the very practice — *sadhana*. As a house holder — *grihastha,* too, this approach is a *sadhana*. As a parent you know the hardship of bringing up a child well. Then he may say, 'You, as a parent never understand my problem.' As a young child he did not know how to even get into the chores associated with bathroom on his own and clean himself. But now after receiving all love and care, he tells the parents, 'You do not know my problem.'

In such a scenario, you as a parent need to know that your happiness is not dependent on his utterance, but try to give your best shot at a given situation and leave it at that. Sometimes, it wonders me when I look at some parents, how much they look after their children, and how children grow up to be at cross roads with their parents.

Reflect on this story.

There was a beautiful tree and it had the ability to speak. The tree invited a child who was playing nearby, by saying, 'Please come and play with me, I have a lot to offer.' The lonely child was playing with the tree; hugging the tree and the tree hugging the child. This practice continued for some days. Every morning the tree used to wait for the child to come. Then it offered the child, 'I have with me many fruits, eat these fruits, as you feel hungry playing with me'.

When the child grew, he was no more attracted to play with the tree. Still the tree like a loving mother, said, 'Come child, come and play with me', the child-turned-youth replied, 'There is nothing interesting in playing with you'. The tree offered to the child-turned-youth could break its twigs, break its branches and play a popular native game — *gilli danda*. Like a loving parent, like a loving mother, the tree said, 'Break certain portions of me, and play.' So much of motherly love the tree was willing to offer.

But, the child-turned-youth — *'tarunastavattaruni saktah'* was interested in pursuit of young maiden. He had no interest in the tree but was interested in the young maiden. But the tree continued its pursuit. It invited the youth to come and play with it. But the youth spurned the offer by saying, 'You are no more interesting to me. I have grown out of enjoying playing *gilli danda*, I have risen above in what my likings are.'

The loving tree like a true mother renewed its offer to changed circumstances and said, 'I still have something to offer, cut me, make a small boat and by making a boat you can go boating in the river nearby. As a teenager you love rowing.' This youth was excited at this proposal and cut the tree.

This is what most children do.

He then made a beautiful boat and went about boating, chasing a young maiden — *taruni*. Once again he lost interest in the tree. Again the tree like ever loving mother said, 'I have nothing to offer you as you have cut me. Oh, my child, but the vast trunk of me can be a beautiful seat for you to come and sit down. Having rowed the boat in the river, at least come and sit on my trunk. I feel as though you are seated on my lap.'

When I read this simple story, I found that most of the parent's plights are like the tree... giving, giving and more giving. But the children go on taking, taking and taking, and then they say parents don't understand what their problems are. But that is life.

However, hard it may sound but it is a hard reality every parent should be prepared to face. If and when things turn out so, the eternal truths — *Brahma vidya*, you have studied well would come as a rescue. You would realise that every soul has its own journey. All that you can say to yourself is, 'I have done the best for my children. The doing itself was beautiful. The very effort to bring up the children was beautiful. *Udyamo Bhairavaha* — the very effort of bringing up the children as such is *Shiva* — *bhairavaha*, the work of Almighty and is auspicious.

When once such understanding of supreme understanding — *para vidya* dawns, you understand that bringing up the children in itself was beautiful. That activity itself is *Shiva, mangalam*, auspiciousness. The parents may start seeing in the very action itself there is a source of joy.

Therefore, you have to practice the eternal truths — *Brahma vidya*, far more deeply when children do not follow your wishes. When children follow your well meant instructions, advice or wishes, treat them as though it is like an extra bonus in your kingdom of joy and happiness.

Having said that when they do not heed to your advice or follow your good intented instructions, it is also like bonus for you to learn not to be dependent — *paratantram*, on their doings but you be free — *swatantram.*

Thus having understood *brahmacharya* and *grihastha avasthas* and led life fully in the tenements of the disciplines of both the lifestyles, the master invites one to the higher realm of existence. He says life led in these two stages are enough and advices one to embrace and welcome meaningful life in old age — *vaanaprasthaashram.* This is how our *rishis* — sages made the life map, though appropriately one can modify it to suit present day context.

Vaanaprastha is a stage of life that directs one to take shelter in a forest, and lead a life as it shows up in the forest with bare minimum material comfort. The person in *Vaanaprastha* remains all by himself, alone and goes through the life with oneself. But most of us do not even know how to be alone and be with oneself.

One need not go to a forest in a current scenario or else the forest would turn out like our cities but the spirit of this can be practised even being in one's own room. It is like giving oneself a conscious shock of saying enough of responsibilities that are undertaken and lead a life in a state of silence, observation of oneself and notice change within.

Practise by being alone as most of us do not know and are not comfortable just being alone. In *brahmacharya avastha*, it is taught from the *Vedas*, that one has to be an *ekaki* — being alone. In the *Bhagavad Gita*, Lord Krishna advices Arjuna in the battlefield to practice ekaki yatachittatma.

Why should the Lord advice being alone in the battlefield? *Ekaki* means one who is alone. In the context of

Mahabharatha Arjuna had to fight, but the Lord advices on the contrary by saying, 'Be alone.' Why? Because if one is not at peace with oneself, how can one be at peace with all action filled life.

Just imagine that you are a student of music and regularly practising music. The field of music that you have chosen may be flute but you are yet to master the musical notes — *swaraas*, properly. But you desire to play a duet with another musician — *jugalbandi,* who is well versed in the field of playing the traditional drum like instrument — *tabla.* How can you play *jugalbandi* with the tabla musician, when you are not clear about your own *swaraas?* If you were to engage in duet — *jugalbandi,* you have to master the *swaraas,* incorporate the *swara gyan* which means, the knowledge of musical notes through your musical instrument like flute.

When you reach a stage of competence in playing solo numbers you can attempt to play alongside with another artist… that could be a flutist, guitarist or a santurist. And thus, you may produce music of melody and synergy by synthesizing two or more musical instruments in a group.

Similarly, the reason for you being not alone could be something on these lines. Your self shows up as only out of tune — *besur,* and then you get married to a person whose life also shows up as *besur.* The result of such union will only result in increased disharmony.

It is like somebody drowning and screaming for help as he did not know swimming. The person who was on the shore saw him drowning, went out to extend help immediately and jumped into water. The person who jumped did not know swimming either. The person who is drowning did not know swimming and the person who jumped out to extend help did not know swimming.

Both were in water but did not know swimming, then who will help whom? Both will help each other in drowning. This is what happens in most of the marriages.

You do not know how to be with yourself and your spouse do not know to be alone. Both cannot be themselves, both of them start drowning helping each other. This is a chaos most marriages are subjected to. One of the major issues of my counseling focuses handling life when one is alone. People say, 'I am feeling lonely. My husband does not return home on time'.

That is why Lord Krishna advises Arjuna – practice by being alone. But don't run away from the world. Be alone, be in the world. This is one of the reasons why nature gives us a taste of what it means to be in a bliss state everyday by inducing sleep. Just imagine one's life without the benefit of sleep. When in sleep, you are alone, but unconsciously you are alone as you are inactive. But can you experience similar state when you are awake. This is a big question in the life of a person engaged in pursuit of spiritual life — *sadhaka.*

Therefore, it is emphasized on the practice of being alone — *ekaki* and life of *vanaprasthaashram. Vanaprasta ashram* is where you start being alone. You have been with the world all along and now embrace the other dimension of life to be alone. Be at peace with yourself.

The last stage of life is one of detachment from worldly affairs — *sanyaas*. No more preparations required if all the three stages of life are led satisfactorily. One simply floats in the miracles of life thereafter and experiences certain newness which may be difficult even to word them. This is the road map in the path of ultimate good — *shreyas*. The four avasthas are *brahmacharya, grihastha, vaanaprastha and sanyaas*. The whole summary or essence — *taatparya*, is one of ultimate freedom — *nirvana*.

The path of the worldly pursuits — *preyas* is the path of pleasure, where ego — *ahankara* is more cemented in an individual. Ego — *ahankara* is after more power, name, and more fame. Even at the age of ninety, there are some who are in the pursuit of more power, fame and name. The whole body — *angam galitam*, may be shaking but nothing has shaken the bundle of desires — *aasha pindam*. Everything else in the body is shaky... teeth are falling, limbs are shaking, bones are brittle, voice is cracking, eyesights are failing, ears are turning to deafness, the very back bone is bent backwards but still the *aasha pindam* is present in its full glory and not yet diminished.

Such a person is said to be deep rooted in the path of *preyas* – the worldly pursuits. Please understand this is the typical map of those who are in the path of *preyas*, not in the path of *shreyas*.

For example, if you resort to taking drugs on a regular basis as a habit, what would happen? It will lead to many complicated problems. If you are a diabetic and consume as many sweets it will lead to many other problems. The great sages have given a life map for one to practice and lead the life in a most benefitting way for the well-being of one self and to the society. Some exceptions may be there. Once you know this like a crystal you should decide your path of leading meaningful life as if it is a gift of the Almighty.

Adi Shankaracharya further states that the path of ultimate good — *shreyas* leads to the path of inner freedom — *nirvana*, as the essence — *taatparya*. Enlightenment — *Moksha* is the *taatparya*. But the path of worldly pursuits — *preyas* may end up like this. He says *balastavat kridasaktah*, during childhood you are lost in play, just nothing but play.

Playing is not a problem, but getting lost in it creates a problem.

As I told you, if you continue thus, you are childish but not child-like. I am saying this because people have denounced play in our country very badly. *Krida* is play; most of the people have denounced playing by wrong thinking especially in our country.

Not every one but ignorant who do not have a clear life map as discussed above. Why should one not play? No. One should be serious in all the activities of life. Seriously get married, and seriously produce children.

The master says be child-like but not childish. Childlikeness is learning to respond in life, whereas childishness is constantly reacting in life. Please understand the danger of constantly reacting. Some petty differences do exist but one reacts strongly; even on trivial issues one's response is reaction, reactions and more reactions. Thus one creates files of hurt bodies in oneself and the hurt bodies are an invitation to a disaster in the waiting. Such a life invariably turns out miserable. If you are leading such a life, my advice to you is very simple. Immediately, renounce such a life.

Reflect on this example.

A man called his residence and was surprised to hear a strange voice at the other end. He enquired, 'Who is speaking?' The person at the other end said, 'I am Robert. What do you want? Who are you?

The caller, the owner of the house was confused further at the strange happening at his residence asked further, 'I am calling my residence. Where is my wife? I am her husband calling from this end. To add further confusion Robert replied, 'Your wife is taking bath.'

The caller was upset as he could not recognise the reply which was in a male voice; he felt his wife was having an affair. He fumed and thundered, 'I shall give you two lakh of rupees if you cut her into two pieces, please kill her and cut her into two pieces'.

The man, Robert at the other end said, 'I will do anything for money.' He asked the caller to wait for a while, then went in and killed the lady as advised on phone, came back to the receiver and said, 'Yes. I have killed her. What next?'

The caller further instructed Robert that there was a lake nearby and he could dispose the body by throwing the cut body away.

Robert in utter confusion said, 'Boss, there is no lake at all next to the house, there are only plenty of apartment buildings all around. Which lake are you talking of?' The caller shockingly asked again, 'Is this number 6408777?' Robert replied, 'Sorry Boss, it is not 6408777, it is a wrong number.'

This may sound a bit exaggerated but I am trying to say how quickly one reacts. There are several incidents that occur before our eyes and we watch many things around us. But quickly we react to everything. We seem to have an opinion on what we know, what we do not know, what others ought to know and what others do not know... the list is endless.

The fact is, showing reaction to everything that occurs around us has become a way of our life. I want to give you a new definition — childishness is reacting, childlikeness is responding. Child-likeness is being innocent, childishness is being arrogant. So therefore, please make an effort to drop childish behaviour.

Most of our reactions, if you look at them closely, come from our past. There is a known structure of the past and our life treads on the known path. So our attachment becomes a storehouse of chaos. In such a chaos, all our attachments in various forms make our lives miserable.

Patanjali in his *Yogasutra* says, from the ego — *ahankaara*, one has to raise oneself to innocence — *asmita*, and from the egoistic 'I' one should transform like an innocent 'I'. When one reaches that state, action emerging out of innocence is very different and worthy of emulation.

Reflecting on the life map again, *balastavat krida saktah* then tarunastavattaruni saktah, vrddhastavaccinta *saktah*... the master adds in *vrddhasta*, one would have built up, as I explained earlier, a rigid frame work and perspective of the definition of life... being over cautious about what energy one has built up over the years. The child-likeness is destroyed, prejudices are increased and with this one knows one can never be free and flowing in the company of people.

So, therefore, they constantly engage themselves in worry — *vaccintasaktah*. Who then strives in the path of realising the Truth — *parame brahmani kopi na saktah*. Very few realises. Most do not even enquire what Truth is. If life were to go thus without the basic enquiry, such a life would be a case of a sure failure. The map of worldly pursuit — *preyas* and the map of ultimate good — *shreyas* are there before us. One has to decide on a choice that one wants to adopt as a life style.

Our sages remind us constantly one has to learn to listen — *pounena shravanam kuryaat*. However, because of our ignorance, which is like highly condensed milk not full of sugar but bitterness, it will not easily leave our system. Therefore, again he says who is your wife — *ka te kanta*, because the understanding resides only in the conscious mind. It is not perculating to the subconscious mind due to the presence of ignorance that exists in the subconscious mind.

The conscious mind comprehends easily because it is made up of only one layer, therefore it is easier to grasp; however, going deeper is a difficult task like walking on a rough terrain. And yet again, the master gives a stroke by asking who is your wife – *ka te kanta*.

Even this, if you do not understand, he gives another shot to quell one's ignorance by asking who your son is. Who your child is – *kaste putrah*, this samsara appears as though it is tremendously strange – *vichitra*. Isn't it? — *Samsaroyamativa vicitrah*.

I would like to unfold this abstract in a simple anecdote. A man's and a woman's relationship are indeed very interesting. As a Kannada poet beautifully said, 'Mangoes grow in the plains, top of a terrain, or even on a mountain but salt is dormant in the ocean. The mango and salt when joined together through the art of cookery turn into a tasty and mouth watering pickle. What a great mystery of existence?'

Similarly, a youth, hailing from a non descriptive place somewhere in Kumbhakonam and a maiden from snow capped valley of mountains of Kashmir, join together into a wedlock and vow to each other, 'Without you, I cannot exist.' It appears as though each one is oxygen to other for their survival. They are not born together. During the interplay of events in life one meets the other. So the master is asking the question, who is your wife? Who is your child? – *ka te kanta, kaste putrah*.

One may say, 'As you know, my child is born out of me.' The child is born out of you no doubt, but still the master is asking, 'Who is your child?' Did you create a life? You find a life force flowing through you. In fact, it is the gift of the Divine and it is not your gift. You cannot even make a claim of such a gift. Where is your choice? What have you produced? Are you the architect of this wonderful creation of life? It has happened to you by default of grace, not by your own design.

Get this fact clearly and in no ambiguous terms. In return on your part there is a display of higher arrogance when you boast about saying, 'My son, My daughter...' In reality you find the life forces flow through you which is indeed the gift of the Divine. Consciously however you may try, you cannot even add one strand of a moustache, or eliminate anything from this body. You can eliminate, may be, even a strand of hair only shaving it off. What are you? You cannot do a thing. Nothing is yours. A child has happened in your life. That is it.

This is one of the reasons why Muslims say, God willing it happens — *Insha Allah*, or Hindus say, Lord's Wish — *Hari Icchcha*.

When you guide and operate all your actions through a deep sense of gratitude — *kritajnya bhavana*, your whole perception of life shows up very differently.

> *Ka Te kanta Kaste Putrah*
> *Samsaroyamativa Vicitrah*

So this *samsara* is strange — *vicitrah*. Else somewhere, Adi Shankaracharya beautifully unfolds that one's life is like a bark of plantain tree; when you start peeling the plantain bark, one by one it starts disappearing and ends up in void — *samsaro kadali stambhaavat*.

The master wants us to see this distinction clearly.

VERSE 8

Who is your wife? Who is your son?
Who are you? When does grace dawn?

का ते कान्ता कस्ते पुत्र:
संसारोऽयमतीव विचित्र: ।
कस्य त्वं क: कुत आयात:
तत्त्वं चिन्तय तदिह भ्रात: ।।
(भज-गोविन्दं... भज-गोविन्दं) (८)

Ka Te kanta Kaste Putrah
Samsaroyamativa Vicitrah
Kasya Tvam Kah Kuta Ayatah
Tattvam Cintaya Tadiha Bhratah
(Bhaja-Govindam Bhaja-Govindam...) (8)

का – who is, ते – your, कान्ता – wife, क: – who is, ते – your,
पुत्र: – son, संसार: अयं – this samsaara, अतीव – supremely,
विचित्र – (indeed) wonderful, कस्य – of whom, त्वम् – are you,
क: (त्वम्) – who are you, कुत: – from where, तत्वं – you,
आयात: – have come, तत्वं – of that truth, चिन्तय – reflect/
think, तद् इह – that here alone, भ्रात: – Oh, Brother!, भज –
Seek, गोविन्दं – Govinda

*Who is your wife? Who is your son? Very wonderful indeed is this
samsara. Who are you? From where have you come? Oh, Brother!
Reflect on that truth here. (Seek Govinda, seek Govinda).*

The style of unfoldment of the great saint Adi Shankaracharya is something to take note of. He is flexible. He doesn't unfold like a teacher but instead says, Oh! Brother, — Oh! *Bhratah*, please see what is this *essence*? It is the life force — *Chintaya*. What is the Truth? The Truth of it is something profound; it requires subtle understanding. If you understand the Truth, you find that a realisation that occurs as nothing is mine, 'I am only an instrument, and I am only a *nimitta*.'

Once you know, 'I am only an instrument, nothing is mine.' Then you would be grateful to what you have. You will be thankful to the gifts that came your way and the gifts that went out of your way. Whatever comes welcome it and whatever goes don't hanker after it — *Aagate swagatham kuryaat gachchantam na nivarayet*. Develop this detachment — *vyraagya bhavana*.

So, finally the master leads one to the quintessence of teaching as *detachment* — *vyraagya*. It is said, '*jnaana bhakti vyraagya sidhyartham ahamidaam poojaam karishye...* Develop detachment — *vyragya*.

Once you develop detachment — *vyragya,* towards all those so called near and dear ones, a new perception in you opens. Such a perception would facilitate you to look life afresh with gratitude at your spouse, at your children and others. A new thinking in you would arise that reverberates, 'My spouse is just a gift that existence or nature has bestowed upon me.'

Heart filled with gratitude will enable you to help living life on the guidelines of the map of the sages. Slowly but

surely you would discover life with many wonderful
flavours. Who knows, this very difference would be a new
turning point towards transformation. But operate from
trust.

Please close your eyes. From your heart connect to your
heart, feel as though you don't have a head, just feel your
heart, let Adi Shankaracharya's message flow into your
heart and sow these words of wisdom. Listen totally from
your heart.

Ka Te kanta Kaste Putrah

Samsaroyamativa Vicitrah

Kasya Tvam Kah Kuta Ayatah

Tattvam Cintaya Tadiha Bhratah

(Bhaja-Govindam Bhaja-Govindam…)

Please open your eyes. Let the understanding sink deeply
and penetrate into your heart centre. Let the understanding
remove the ignorance of 'who I am.' *'Tattvam cintaya tadiha
bhratah.' Chintaya* here means thinking faculty of oneself.
What is it that you have to think? 'Who am I?' The master
questions, 'Who your wife is, who your son is and who this
is?'

All these are simple and you seem to know. But you do not
seem to know the *one* who is the knower. You know your
wife, you know your children and you say you know
worldly things, but who is the *knower* of all these is
something you do not know. If you do not know who the
knower is, all that knowing is emerging from your core
ignorance.

So therefore, Ramana Maharishi, the great enlightened master advised whoever came to him, 'Find out who you are?' Somebody came to him and said, 'I have lot of problems. He listened to him and said, 'Find out who has got the problem?' One person, I think from Hyderabad came and told him, 'Please don't tell me to find out who has the problem, because I have come with lots of problems, and I want a quick answer.' Ramana Maharishi answered, 'Find out who is telling, don't ask me to find out who am I.'

Please listen carefully. We seem to know everything around us. I am not saying we know everything for sure, but our energies are always directed on the outer world of objects.

The *Kathopanishad* unfolds wonderfully, '*paraanchi kaani vytrnat swayambhuhu, tasmat paraan pashyati antaraatman.*' Our Upanishad declares that the ordinary trait of the human mind is engaging itself in the objects of the outer world. '*Paranchikaani....* by constantly being focused outwards — *vytrnat*, one is destroyed', it summarises. One has practically destroyed one's core self by being focused on the outer, the world of objects.

The famous teaching of great Ramana Maharishi is, 'Find out who you are'. Adi Shankaracharya is unfolding in a different tonality of the similar essence. Please think over and see — *tadiha bhratah chintaya*, are you just the manifestation of your body? You say, 'I am the body', but the body is constantly changing, you are just observing the changes that the body undergoes.

Hence, the body is observed and you are the observer. Extending this logic further, if you are the thoughts and you watch that the thoughts are emerging and disappearing. Hence, the thoughts are observed and you are the observer.

Thus, your thoughts come and go and they constantly surface and dissolve. It is observed and you are the observer. Fair enough, it is clear till now. But the major question to think as per the master is — who is the observer, observing the observed?

The clarion call to all of us from Ramana Maharishi is — 'Find out who am I.' Yet lovingly he unfolds, that one can reach upto this point through one's *sadhana* and one's monumental effort can take one thus far... to an unquestionable understanding that, 'I am not the body, I am not the mind, I am not the intellect, I am not the thoughts, and I am not the ignorance.'

Why? It is because you are the observer of the body, the observer of the mind, the observer of the thought, the observer of your thoughts and ignorance. Now carefully come in touch with that important dimension of 'Who is this 'I' in all these observation?' 'Who is 'I' that is observing the observed?'

Observe the observer. Put in effort to know the knower. Who knows the known? I agree that up to this point effort can lead you; you cannot probably go beyond this point. You are just an observer, be there in the present... totally.

Water boils at 100 degrees centigrade. So all your spiritual effort is to reach you up to this point, 'I am the observer observing all these happenings.' Be there totally. This is the time for grace to descend on you. Only then, you will be able to see the beyond.

From the famous book *'Tripura Rahasya'* Ramana Maharishi, unfolds that the observer is in consciousness, the observed is in consciousness, the observation is consciousness; and this consciousness has no form and hence, it is formless, and therefore, it cannot be destroyed.

Whatever has form can be destroyed and whatever has no form cannot be destroyed. All this may appear as theory and fit for academic or scholarly debate. The fact is — we have to come to a point that constantly we have to remind ourselves to observe, 'The body is seen, thoughts are seen, I am the observer, my attachment is seen, but who is the person who is having the attachment?'

Slowly discover that person and if you pursue persistently, you would see the seer in and through all these. That is all that you can do. Then it is some other forces that take over and lead you to the pathway of enlightenment. If this were not to happen, be assured that you are engaging in the activities of the outer world without really knowing who you are.

Therefore, the words of the master that invites us to, *'tattvam cintaya tadiha bhratah'*, Oh! Brother, Oh! Bhratah, think deeply as to 'Who you are.'

A monk – *sanyasi*, sits on the seat of meditation and thinks who he is. A house holder — *grihasta*, like all of you, in and through all your activities, just as you take rest, so too whenever you are free sit down, pause and look at 'Who I am' and 'What is *ka te kanta, kaste putrah*', you slowly discover who you are.

In such a space of understanding, you would be grateful to your spouse, to your children. And heart filled with gratitude and you thus start leading and living life. Then you realise the world as, '*Ishaavaasyam idagum sarvam yat kinchit jagatyaam jagat*' and the whole world becomes a Divine play.

In this process the Truth is discovered. Then you will see what is as '*what is*' or else we don't see what is as '*what is.*' '*What is*' becomes a projection of '*what should be*' and therefore we do not see '*what is*' as '*what is*'. We project on '*what is*' through our ignorant mind. How many of us can see *what is* '*as is*'.

An ignorant mind goes on projecting and sees only the objects as forms and it does not see the formless. It is like you stop at the window. Your gaze or sight never passes through the window. When you look at the sky through the window, you think the sky is limited to the size of the window, because your sight is limited to the window. Therefore, all distorted perception starts happening.

Adi Shankaracharya adds further, 'First think'. If you are drunk and you enquire, it is drunken state enquiry. Come out of the drunken state and enquire.

When the drunken state of the mind disappears you see who you really are. Once you see who you are, you perceive *what is* '*as is*'. Then your inner eyes becomes windows of perception, your inner eyes will not distort perception. That's the state of clarity the master is inviting us to.

He further states for such clarity to dawn in an individual,

VERSE 9

This is the way. This is the path.
This is the direction. This is the destination

सत्सङ्गत्वे निस्सङ्गत्वं
नि:सङ्गत्वे निर्मोहत्वम् ।
निर्मोहत्वे निश्चलतत्त्वं
निश्चलतत्त्वे जीवन्मुक्ति: ।।
(भज-गोविन्दं... भज-गोविन्दं) (९)

Satsangatve Nissangatvam
Nihsangatve Nirmohatvam
Nirmohatve Niscalatattvam
Niscalatattve Jivanmuktih
(Bhaja-Govindam Bhaja-Govindam...) (9)

सत् सङ्गत्वे – through the company of the wise, निस्सङ्गत्वं – (there arises) non-attachment, नि:सङ्गत्वे – through non-attachment, निर्मोहत्वम् – (there arises) freedom from delusion, निर्मोहत्वे – through the freedom from delusion, निश्चल – unchangeable, तत्त्वं – reality, निश्चलतत्त्वे – through the immutable reality, जीवन्मुक्ति: – (comes) the state of liberation or freedom, भज – Seek, गोविन्दं – Govinda

Through the company of the wise, (there arises) non-attachment. Through non-attachment (there arises) freedom from delusion, when there is freedom from delusion, there is the unchangeable reality. On experiencing unchangeable reality, there comes liberation or freedom. (Seek Govinda, seek Govinda).

He is offering a new road map to the seeker.

You listen constantly the words of the great seers. It is very important to be in the company of the wise — *satsanga*. More than the words, it is their presence, more than the logic, it is their love, more than the structure of the path, it is the structure-less understanding as understanding has no structure that is going to make a deep impact and difference in the life of a seeker. If you observe closely, a thought has a structure. You try to comprehend something that does not conform to a structure through a structure of thought.

Therefore, be in the company of the wise — *satsanga*. Being constantly in the company of the wise — *satsanga* gives you solitude — *nissanga,* from *nissanga* delusion — *nirmoha,* will lose its grip over you, when *nirmoha,* void of delusion happens, *niscalatattvam* — unchangeable reality surfaces, then *niscalatattve jivanmuktih* – one realises the state of liberation.

Jivan means living. Don't nurse a feeling that after death you will be transported to the heavenly abode — *vaikunta.* While living itself, in this very life convert your life of deficiency — *samsaara,* into a state of inner freedom — *nirvana.* Or else, the reverse would happen... you may convert *nirvana* into *samsara.* So, it is vital to be in the association of the wise — *satsanga*.

When you constantly listen you know what happens? It is like cleaning the mirror.

Reflect on this incident.

A master — *guru* taught the disciple — *shishya* all that

he knew of. Having taught all the scriptures, he told the disciple that for the final teaching he would have to go to a nearby ashram.

He said, 'There is another *guru* from whom you will learn the final teachings.' The disciple was in a state of confusion and wonderment. His thoughts went reasoning like this — 'My *guru* is more knowledgeable. How can the other *guru* be more knowledgeable than my *guru*?' He was aware of the limited reputation of the *guru* in the nearby ashram as far as his knowledge was concerned.

The disciple was in two minds... to go or not. Trusting the words of his *guru* he set out to meet the other *guru* in the nearby ashram. To his utter surprise his new found *guru* had stopped teaching. He found that the new found *guru* was only serving food to everybody in the ashram out of love.

The *guru* himself would cook and would serve, not only that, the *guru* himself would clean the left overs and wash the dishes.

So the disciple saw how lovingly the *guru* was serving and he understood what it meant to serve out of love. Later he noticed something profound. The *guru* himself washed the dishes and kept them in order before he went to sleep.

Next morning, he used to take out the dishes, washed them again and started cooking. The disciple was wondering as to why the *guru* should wash the dishes all over again in the morning while they were already been washed thoroughly earlier in the night and that dishes were not dusty either. He observed all such details and came back to narrate to his earlier *guru*.

He narrated, 'I cannot understand this strange fact of why should the *guru* in the nearby ashram wash the already cleaned vessels again in the morning, why should he do that?'

To which his *guru* replied, 'Yes, this is the understanding that I wanted you to observe and get totally.'

You cleanse your mind regularly but your mind start collecting dust along the way in form of a clutter, foggy and unclear understanding. Please do not say that you do meditation once and stop at that. So long as your mind gathers dust it has to be cleansed.

Thus, it has to be an ongoing process. You have to go on purifying the mind.

Therefore, there is a mention of *asakrit upadesha. Asakrit* means until you understand. Constantly listen. Go on listening till you are one with the understanding — *Pounena shravanam kuriyat.*

So, the company of the wise — *satsanga* will give you solitude — *nissanga*. More you are in the company of wise — *satsanga,* you develop detachment. When detachment takes place, your delusion gets washed away. When delusion gets washed way, you start realising the Truth. Once you know the Truth, you lose the grip on life of deficiency — *samsaara* in spite of being in *samsaara*.

This is the way. This is the path. This is the direction. This is the destination.

And therefore, '*Bhaja Govindam, Bhaja Govindam,* Govindam Bhaja mudhamate. Samprapte sannihite *kale na hi na hi raksati dukrn karane.*' Seek Govinda, seek Govinda. Oh! Fool, grammar-rules are not going to protect you at the time when death haunts and finally arrives. All these are not going to protect you. Your wife is not going to protect you, your husband is not going to protect you and your children will not protect you even though they are wonderful company to be with.

It is only the ultimate truth — *Brahma Vidya* that will protect you. So give priority and importance in realising that Truth. If you understand this very clearly you direct the ship of your life wisely or else you go down drowning in life.

VERSE 10

Ways to conquer inner deficiency

वयसि गते क: कामविकार:
शुष्के नीरे क: कासार: ।
क्षीणे वित्ते क: परिवारो
ज्ञाते तत्त्वे क: संसार: ।।
(भज-गोविन्दं... भज-गोविन्द) (१०)

Vayasi Gate Kah Kamavikarah
Suske Nire Kah Kasarah
Ksine Vitte Kah Parivaro
Jnate Tattve Kah Samsarah
(Bhaja-Govindam Bhaja-Govindam...) (10)

वयसि गते (सति) – when the age (youthfulness) has passed,
क: – where is, कामविकार: – lust and its modification/play,
शुष्के नीरे (सति) – when water is evaporated (dried up),
क: – where is, कासार: – the lake, क्षीणे वित्ते (सति) – when the
wealth is reduced, क: – where is, परिवार – the retinue, ज्ञाते तत्त्वे
(सति) – when the truth is realised, क: – where is, संसार: – the
samsara, भज – Seek, गोविन्दं – Govinda

*When youth has passed, where is lust and its modification/play? When
water has evaporated where is the lake? When wealth is reduced where is
the retinue? When the truth is realised where is samsara – a state of
inner deficiency? (Seek Govinda, seek Govinda).*

When the age of youthfulness has passed where is lust and its play? When water is evaporated, where is the lake? When the wealth is reduced, where are the attendants? When truth is realised, where is *samsara?*

Seek Govinda, Seek Govinda.

Attachment is when one declares to oneself, 'Without this, I refuse to be happy'. These attachments are our inner conclusions and these conclusions drive our lives. The driver of our inner life is controlled by them. We have to inspect, audit and edit to bring correctness into our lives. Error in thinking brings error in feelings and thus error in feelings brings error in actions and hence, we are led to an inner state of deficiency — *samsara.*

We feel a sense of deficiency thinking there is something lacking in the world of objects which we do not possess. If we do not possess money or power or position or sex life, and thus strong inner conclusions that we draw upon ourselves drives us to purse them vigorously. Unconsciously, we walk into the unknown trap and get hooked on to them.

If one begins to observe oneself through the teaching of enlightened masters like Adi Shankacharya, one begins to observe deeply one's life with reference to higher teachings and come in touch with the culprit called attachment and mechanical driven-ness to the world of objects.

It is not what we know which makes a difference but how deeply we know which makes a difference. Our knowledge should impact our 'Being', and then it is true growth. Or it is nothing but ignorance parading as knowledge. The depth of knowledge happens when one observes one's life with a deep rooted commitment to transform oneself.

When we observe deeply, we find more than the lack of money, power, position, name and fame... it is our poor 'state of Being' that we genuinely strive for. If one's level of 'Being' is low, it is an invitation to entertain oneself with imagination of something totally wrong or opposite.

It is wrong to say, 'it is nothing but imagination.' Imagination is power. It is a well acknowledged mental faculty that one can be endowed with. But when one imagines something other than the reality of a given situation it supplements one's feeling of deficiency. Imaginations can play havoc in one's life.

So, it is all the more necessary to work on the level of one's 'Being.' One's 'Being' is enhanced by true understanding and devotion, and detachment to illusions which makes us get wrongly attached. In that enhanced state of 'Being', one sees life in a sacred space.

Oscar Wilde said, 'Oh youth, what a pity it is wasted on the young.' When you are young, you have energy but no maturity and when you are old, you may have maturity but no energy.

Bring both youth and maturity in your life.

'When the age has passed where is lust and its play?'

During youth one's body is well equipped to stir lustful cravings and as one advances in age the virility drops, and the urge for sexual intimacy wanes away. In fact, it is a natural process of one being attracted to the member of the opposite sex. It does not pose a problem as such.

But the imaginary self in one concludes and creates an attachment to an illusion that sex is everything in life. It is such illusion born out of imagination and created by conclusion that has to be dropped.

Adi Shankaracharya, the great master provides us with many examples to drop our illusions. If we see closely we cannot drop an illusion, we have to bring in the light of understanding. We cannot remove darkness unless we bring in light. The master lights our being with clarity through these examples.

'When wealth is reduced, where is the attendant?'

The mass of humanity is mechanically driven by illusions. When one has wealth, people hanker around. But one has an illusion that people are around because of the person. It is far from truth. People are attached to money and one who has money is surrounded by people.

Sooner one comes in touch with this reality the better for the individual's spiritual growth. Ultimately, if one's state of 'Being' is on a wiser path of understanding one would be able to see this clearly. This clarity would help one deal with life not mechanically but from a magnetic center of understanding.

'When Truth is realised where am I in the life of dependency – *samsara?*'

Truth liberates one while illusions binds one. Truth is we see *what is*, '*as is*'. '*What is*' is always full. But with the aid of our ego and its imaginary self, we see *what* we want to see.

We don't see *'what is'* as *'what is.'* *'What is'* is always complete, but a 'thought' intervenes and says, 'no, I want this' and this 'thought' make us feel incomplete and not *'what is as is.'*

See the truth of *'what is'* and drop the illusion of *'what should be.'* In such a state you experience fullness in the *now* and not in the *future.*

This fullness is dropping a sense of deficiency — *samsara.*

VERSE 11

Pride and illusions — chains that bind

मा कुरु धनजनयौवनगर्व
हरति निमेषत्काल: सर्वम् ।
मायामयमिदमखिलं बुद्ध्व
ब्रह्मपदं त्वं प्रविश विदित्वा ॥
(भज-गोविन्दं... भज-गोविन्दं) (११)

Ma Kuru Dhananjayauvanagarvam
Harati Nimesatkalah Sarvam
Mayamayamidamakhilam Buddhva
Brahmapadam Tvam Pravisa Viditva
(Bhaja-Govindam Bhaja-Govindam...) (11)

मा – do not, कुरु – take, धन – in wealth/position, जन – in the people, यौवन – in youth, गर्व – pride, हरति – snatches, निमेषात् – in a moment, काल: – the time, सर्व – all these, मायामयं – full of illusory nature, इंद – this, अखिलं – all, बुद्ध्वा – after understanding, ब्रह्मपदं – the state of Brahman, त्वं – you, प्रविश – enter into, विदित्वा – after realising, भज – Seek, गोविन्दं – Govinda

Take no pride in your wealth, in people, in the youthfulness. Time snatches away all these in a moment. All these are illusions, after understanding this; enter into the state of Brahman. (Seek Govinda, seek Govinda).

'Take no pride in your possessions.'

When one achieves something, one need not feel proud about such achievements. A true spiritual person is one who feels grateful of his successes or achievements.

If one is successful, it is due to the Divine laws and nothing to do with one's egoistic will. If one is a good speaker, the vocal chord is not created by anyone but one is blessed by the laws of nature or the Lord. If one can remember and quote many things during a speech, it is the work of a brain not created by anyone but one is endowed by existence... which is nothing but the work of Lord.

Indeed, one has to grateful to all that one is endowed with rather than feeling proud about.

It is certainly wrong to feel proud whether one is rich, or young or one has many friends... feeling proud is a mere excuse of being egoistic.

The real culprit is that one's ego is always waiting for some excuses to throw out its foolishness and inner toxicity.

Arrogance is an expression of a symptom where energies within oneself which are disorganized. A disorganized inner development has ego as its general and it throws out arrogance.

One has to be aware of the games of ego. Its ways can be gross or subtle. A spiritual seeker should catch it right and not allow them to rule one's life. If you throw it out from one door, it enters through another. Its ways are subtle and manipulative. Beware of its presence. Its presence is the absence of goodness.

The foolish idea of renunciation — *sanyas*, is leaving the world but the true meaning is renouncing one's ego and its arrogance.

If one is truly living a conscious life and not a life of sleep-fullness, one will realise that, 'time snatches away all these… money, youth, power and people in a second', says the great Adi Shankaracharya.

If all these are changing, there must be a changeless principle and the great Adi Shankaracharya invites us to enter into this world of enlightenment. Life's higher purpose is to search for that state of 'Being' — enlightenment.

'See the illusory nature of the world.'

The world is not an illusion as such but the way you see the world is an illusion. You see the world filled with your desires, expectations, upsets, and unhappy memories. Then you superimpose on the objective world your subjective garbage and thus live in subjective creation — *jiva sritshti*, and not in the Lord's world — *iswara sritsti*.

'Realise the state of Brahman and enter into it', he says in this verse.

Man's journey appears to be in the following order:

From one state of unhappiness to another state of unhappiness like one getting into wrong habits of smoking, drinking…

Second stage is from state of unhappiness to state of happiness… seeking right ways to be happy.

The third stage is from state of happiness to state of happiness. He now gets into another trap of seeking more happiness and gets lost in wanting more happiness.

The last and wise stage is, from a state of happiness to no ego and the state of *Brahman*... that of *Brahmapadam* where one can stand face to face with truth and that too as an inner experience. Such an experience where there is no subject but pure experience. These are not just words but a content which cannot be contained by any words.

Pride strengthens the ego and to drop this pride is to weaken the ego. To see the world *as it is* and not influenced by the ego is being in the right path to enlightenment.

VERSE 12

Interplay of seasons, time and desires

दिनयमिन्यौ सायं प्रातः ।
शिशिरवसन्तौ पुनरायातः ।
कालः क्रीडति गच्छत्ययुः
तदपि न मुञ्चत्यशावायुः ।।
(भज-गोविन्दं... भज-गोविन्दं) (१२)

Dinayaminyau Sayam Pratah
Sisiravasantau Punarayatah
Kalah Kridati Gacchatyayuh
Tadapi Na Muncatyasavayuh
(Bhaja-Govindam Bhaja-Govindam...) (12)

दिनयमिन्यौ – in day and night, सायं – evening, प्रातः – morning, शिशिरवसन्तौ – winter and spring, पुनः – again, आयतः – come (and depart), कालः – time, क्रीडति – plays, गच्छति – give away (goes away), आयुः – life (breath), तदपि – and yet, न – not, मुञ्चति – leaves, आशा वायुः – the gust of desire, भज – Seek, गोविन्दं – Govinda

Day and night, evening and morning, winter and spring, again and again come (and goes). Time plays and life goes away. And yet one leaves not the gusts of desires. (Seek Govinda, seek Govinda).

'Day and night, dusk and dawn, winter and spring come again and again and depart. Time sports and life ebbs away, and yet one leaves not the gust of desires.'

People whose main worry is — their own happiness and that too seeking outside themselves and riding on the horse of desire, do not find it.

To be happy one foolishly adds possessions, but the wise subtract from desires and finds happiness within themselves.

Full devotion to the Lord puts anxiety to rest and hence seek that Lord, seek the Lord.

'Yet one leaves not the gust of desires.'

There are two types of desires. One is a desire to 'become happy' while the other is a 'desire out of happiness'. What entraps us is the desire to become happy. The desire to become happy becomes the conclusion that one is not happy. Such a conclusion is insane. In the state of deep sleep one is happy without desires and without any material achievement. Where did this happiness come from? Hence happiness is within us and is present in the *now.*

But the desiring mind lives in the *future.* The future does not exist at all; for even if the future happens, it happens in the present. The past was present, the present is present and the future will also be the present. So the present is the real basis of time, even though time is past, present and future.

A desiring mind lives in the future and discards the

present. To live in the present is true wisdom and sanity. To live in the present, one has to drop the desiring mind that takes one into the future. Desires in a nutshell means to many, 'Only if this happens I will become happy'.

In such a scenario, you are sacrificing the present for the future.

Desires are like being mad. They make you mad in two ways. If they are fulfilled you will feel that you have been running after some shadow and thus you desire something more.

And if they are not fulfilled you will feel frustrated.

All desires are foolish and true wisdom is 'in being desire-less'.

'Day and night, dusk and dawn, winter and spring, again and again come and depart.'

The world is changing, time is moving on, everything in life is impermanent, but the unwise seek something permanent in the impermanent.

One has to observe one's seeking, question one's seeking. Or else, one mechanically seeks. If one's life is mechanical in seeking, in living, and in thinking, one destroys the core of oneself and that is — one is a 'conscious being'.

In spite of one's core being consciousness one lives a mechanical life. This is something like death. One need to address this aspect in one's living and seeking. The world and time are impermanent, and one is mechanically seeking permanence in the impermanent.

Spiritual life is to notice one's unawareness and become more aware. Then one's 'state of being' would change. When one's 'state of being' changes, one's perception and meaning that one gives to life will not be mechanical but will come from a higher or a greater source.

Then one would not ride on desires but live in the present with deep devotion. One experiences sacredness and see sacredness all around. One experiences the Divine presence everywhere. For this understanding to happen, one's 'state of being' has to change from desire oriented living to devotional oriented living.

Reflect on this story.

A fanatic Christian and not a true Christian converted a Hindu Brahmin by teaching him the bible. The scholarly Hindu went on appreciating the teaching and said, 'These are words of an enlightened soul'.

This Christian missionary was filled with boundless joy.

On the way back to his church, he found Jesus standing by the roadside rock. 'Oh, Lord! I have converted a scholarly Hindu Brahmin', he said.

Jesus smiled and said, 'I see this has only enhanced your ego.'

VERSE 13

Distinction of the path of wordly pursuits and goodness

का ते कान्ता धनगतचिन्ता
वातुल किं तव नास्ति नियन्ता ।
त्रिजगति सज्जनसंगतिरेका
भवति भवार्णवतरणे नौका ।।
(भज-गोविन्दं... भज-गोविन्दं) (१३)

Ka Te Kanta Dhanagatacinta
Vatula Kim Tava Nasti Niyanta
Trijagati Sajjanasangatireka
Bhavati Bhavarnavatarane Nauka
(Bhaja-Govindam Bhaja-Govindam...) (13)

का – where is, ते – your, कान्ता – wife, धनगत – pertaining to wealth, चिन्ता – worry, वातुल – o distracted one, किं – is there, तव – to you, न अस्ति – not, नियन्ता – the ordainer of rules (one who ordains or commands), त्रिजगति – in the three worlds, सज्जन – of the wise, संगति – association, सज्जन संगति – the association with the wise, एका – alone, भवति – becomes (can serve as), भव अर्णव तरणे – to cross the sea of change (birth and death), नौका – the boat, भज – Seek, गोविन्दं – Govinda

Oh, distracted one! Why worry about wife, wealth...? Is there not for you the one who ordains? In the three worlds it is the association with wise people alone that can serve as a boat to cross the sea of change — Samsara. (Seek Govinda, seek Govinda).

'Oh, distracted one, why worry about wife, wealth and so on..., is there not for you the one who ordains? In the three worlds it is the association with the good people alone that can serve as a boat to cross the sea of change... birth and death.'

Seek Govinda, seek Govinda.

'Oh, distracted one.'

The master lovingly hits at the ignorant by saying, 'Oh distracted one.' Most are distracted as they have lost the true purpose of life. Their life is like a drift. There are two paths one can choose according to the *Vedas*

(a) Preyas

(b) Shreyas

The path of *preyas* is the path of pleasures, fame, name, power, position or in other words: ego filled pursuits.

The path of *shreyas* is the path of the ultimate good, of the enlightened, the path of innocence and not arrogance. One has to choose the path of ultimate goodness — *shreyas* and not the path of worldly pursuits — *preyas* which only leads to glamour and not goodness.

If one does not create consciously the path of goodness - *shreyas,* then one's tendencies would automatically go to ego oriented pursuits — *preyas.* Then by default, one's life will be gravitated to glamour and ego pursuits.

Have you noticed when a person joins a monastery and by default his pattern would be to head the organization? There is a default track laid down by many births in us as we have pursued the path of the ego.

So, one has to put in a great effort, a conscious effort called as *Bhagirath Prayatnam* to be on the track of goodness. *Bhagirath* was a King narrated in the epic *Mahabharatha* who was instrumental in descending the river Ganges to earth from heaven so as to wash away the sins of his forefathers. Such stupendous effort is called *Bhagirath Prayatnam*.

'Why worry about wife or wealth?'

Worry is like a rocking chair, it keeps you busy but leads you no where. To worry is to insult God's wisdom.

This should be the trust by which a devotee should operate. By worrying there is a leakage of energies. When there is a leakage of energies, overflowing is not possible. It is by overflowing energies alone that one can be filled with the mystery of the Divine. One has to learn to drop worrying. If one learns to trust in God and operate out of trust, worry would automatically stop.

Reflect on this story.

After many years of courtship, a person got married. Soon, the newly wed couple had to cross a river. While crossing the river in a boat they encountered a storm. The panic spread around, but this person was highly relaxed and did nothing. His wife screamed at him and said, 'Are you not worried and scared that we may die?'

'No', replied the husband.

'Why and what is the secret of you being so calm?'

He took out his knife at his beloved and screamed, 'I will kill you.'

She was calm. He asked her, 'Why you are not scared?'

She replied, 'The knife may be dangerous but the one who is holding the knife loves me dearly and so I am not scared.'

To which the man replied, 'Similarly, the waves may be turbulent but the Lord who wields the waves loves me and so I am not scared. Whatever he does, I trust he does for our well-being.'

Such trust will uplift one's life and in such a space a person becomes truly spiritual. He believes there is a creator who cares. He operates from an understanding that the creation is intelligent and hence there is an intelligent creator.

Then why do people suffer?

If they encounter difficulties, people interpret it as misery. The problem is about the interpretation. One has to be in the company of the good, and then one will interpret things properly and wisely.

Hence, the master says, 'Association with the good people can serve as a boat to cross the sea of change.'

It is said more often, suffering is a wake up call of existence so that we come out of our sleeping consciousness. We are too comfortable in our sleep. Hence, great sages tell us that suffering is a great gift from the Divine.

See an opportunity in a difficulty and not see difficulty in an opportunity. The company of the wise will make you see an opportunity in a difficulty and it will be like a boat which will help you cross the river of the life of deficiency — *samsara*.

VERSE 14

Ways people undertake for survival needs

जटिलो मुण्डी लुञ्चितकेश:
काषायाम्बरबहुकृत्वेष: ।
पश्यन्नपि च न पश्यति मूढो
ह्युदरनिमित्तं बहुकृत्वेष: ।
(भज-गोविन्दं... भज-गोविन्दं) (१४)

Jatilo Mundi Luncitakesah
Kasayambarabahukrtavesah
Pasyannapi Ca Na Pasyati Mudho
Hyudaranimittam Bahukrtavesah
(Bhaja-Govindam Bhaja-Govindam...) (14)

जटिल: – one ascetic with hair locks, मुण्डी – one with shaven head लुञ्चितकेश – one with hairs pulled out one by one, काषाय अम्बर बहृकृत वेष: – one wearing with ochre robes, पश्यन् अपि च – though seeing, न – never, पश्यति – sees, मूढ: – a fool, हि – indeed, उदर निमित्तं – for belly's sake, बहुकृत वेष: – these different disguises or apparels, भज – Seek, गोविन्दं – Govinda

One ascetic with hair locks, one with shaven head, one with hair pulled out one by one, another wearing saffron robes – these are fools who though seeing, do not see. Indeed different disguises are only for their belly's sake. (Seek Govinda, seek Govinda).

'One ascetic with matted-locks, one with a shaven-head, and one with hair pulled out one by one, another parading in his ochre robes... these are fools who though seeing, do not see. Indeed these different disguises are only for their belly's sake'.

Seek Govinda, Seek Govinda.

Change is of two forms. There is an outer change and there is an inner change. True change is the inner change. Even though the outer change can impact the inner change, but the inner change impacts the outer change more.

This can be narrated by an example.

For the first time in her life, a lady goes to a party in a five star hotel. She feels very happy. The ambience and the grandeur of the hotel are unbelievable for her imagination. But when the other invitees make their presence, all of a sudden she hits a new low. Her mind immediately gets into an inner dialogue creating discomfort such as – the others are best dressed than her, they have decked up with appealing ornaments and she feels very depressed.

What is happening in her mind is a result of the inner impacting... of the mind more than the outer ambience and grandeur of the hotel.

Thus, the Master says that the monks by matted locks, or shaven head or hair being pulled out, these are outer changes and they do not change the core of your inner being. Work on the core of your inner being by seeking the

Lord, seeking the truth.

'Though seeing they do not see.'

This is a great paradox that you see but still you do not see. There are people who are like sleep walkers; they are asleep, their consciousness is asleep but they can walk, eat and still go back to bed without knowing what they have done.

The need for survival is the lowest need. To be enlightened is the greatest need. By fulfilling the greatest need, the lowest need will be fulfilled. '*Hasti pade sarvapadam nimagnam*' is a Sanskrit maxim which says: 'In the foot of an elephant all the other feet are included.' So, if the need is to attain liberation — *moksha* is fulfilled, all the other smaller needs seem to have been fulfilled.

Why should people adopt to such means of trying to dress up as a monk and try to fulfill the survival needs?

One's mind, when not purified with devotion, detachment, and clarity becomes toxic and such toxicity expresses itself through manipulation, untruth, greed, vanity... Just like how when one is not in a good exercise regimen and a good diet, one's body becomes fat. Similarly it is the case with one's mind.

Manipulation is an expression of an impure mind. People are so manipulative that they themselves do not know they are manipulative. This is the height of manipulation. One has to notice and observe how our manipulation exists in our relationships even. Self observation is a great practice.

Self observation when clubbed with devotion purifies

one's mind and such a pure mind will have finer needs of life.

A gross mind has gross needs and a pure mind will have finer needs.

With a pure mind, one will still fulfill the survival need but it will be through good means and not manipulative means. An impure mind distorts the perception of what is right and wrong. With a pure mind one discovers healthy methods to grow up in life. Very few people grow up, most of us grow old. To grow up is adding life to years and to grow old is adding years to life.

These days, quiet a few spiritual leaders adopt glamorous methods to fulfill their needs. Some create pomp and mysticism around them. Some tell their students to spread and market how great their master is and thus hoodwink others. Some appease rich people and please their ego. Thus, their need for survival is easily met.

The methods may vary but underneath all of them is the need for survival through manipulative means. One has to observe them, identify them, discard them, and keep a safe distance from them. So the effort should be to focus all your energies in seeking the Lord, seeking the Truth, and seeking enlightenment.

VERSE 15

Desire — the ultimate hook of the unwise

अङ्गं गलितं पलितं मुण्डं
दशनविहीनं जातं तुण्डम् ।
वृध्दो याति गृहीत्वा दण्डं
तदपि न मुञ्चत्याशापिण्डम् ॥
(भज-गोविन्दं... भज-गोविन्दं) (१५)

Angam Galitam Palitam Mundam
Dasanavihinam Jatam Tundam
Vrddho Yati Grhitva Dandam
Tadapi Na Muncatyasapindam
(Bhaja-Govindam Bhaja-Govindam...) (15)

अङ्गं – the body, गलितं – (has been) deteriorated, पलितं – has turned grey, मुण्डम् – the hair (the head), दशनविहीनं – toothless, जातं – has become, तुण्डम् – mouth, वृध्द – the old man, याति – moves (goes) about, गृहीत्वा – having taken (leaning on), दण्डं – (his) staff, तदपि – even then, न – never, मुञ्चति – leaves, आशापिण्डम् – the bundle of desires, भज – Seek, गोविन्दं – Govinda

The body has been deteriorated. The hair has turned grey. All teeth have fallen down. The old man moves about leaning on his staff. Even then he leaves not the bundle of desires. (Seek Govinda, seek Govinda).

'The body has become worn out. The head has turned grey. The mouth rendered toothless. The old man moves about leaning on his staff. Even then he leaves not the bundle of his desires'.

Seek Govinda, seek Govinda.

The Hindu thought recognizes that there are two basic drives to human actions.

The first coming from the lower nature called *prakrithi* which is basically driven by necessities. *Prakrithi* means the lower nature or material nature, which is found in the visible world.

The other is *purusha*, which means the higher nature that encompasses higher needs which is found in one's soul or consciousness. Life is like a circle. There is a center and there is a periphery. Most of our lives are spent on the periphery and not on the center. We invest our lives on the survival needs. Born out of fear of survival, all our life energies are spent on protecting and fulfilling survival needs.

It is like, if you want to hit a nail on the wall, you need two units of energy but instead you use hundred units of energy, which means you are using unnecessary energy on a small job. This is how most people, who live life on the periphery do and hence the master says, 'Even then he leaves not the bundle of his desires.' The *acharya* pleads us to seek Govinda, the truth or the *purusha*.

The body has become worn out. The head has turned grey...' and still one is immersed in the world of change and does not search the changeless principle on which the phenomenon of change happens.

There are gross needs and finer needs, the need of the *prakriti* and the need of the *purusha*. If one has not lived a life of devotion — *bhakti*, and true knowledge — *jnana*, one will not recognize the finer needs of life.

You have to fulfill both the needs, but discarding the finer needs of life that is enlightenment, you are like the ship in the ocean without a compass.

The earth pulls you downwards, the worldly needs pull you downwards while the sky invites you upwards, the spiritual need invites you upwards. It appears you are in a conflict. Yes, in a way you are in conflict but if you can be in harmony with the conflict you will create a way to fulfill both.

The out-going breath appears in conflict with the incoming breath, for 'out' is in conflict with 'in'. In fact, 'breathing in' helps you to 'breathe out'. They are not in conflict but they are complementing each other. This is the paradox and mystery of life.

Your logical mind cannot understand the mystery of life. Start your life with logic but do not end your life with logic. Let the loving heart guide to see the poetry and mystery of life. Seek the Lord and let his grace be a spiritual ladder for you to grow and be inwardly free, or you will be tied down with your desires in spite of your body failing you.

If you do not understand this you will remain in pain,

despair, agony, and the Divine ecstasy will be lost and it will not have an appointment in your life.

One lives in despair because one's mind mechanically lives in desires and hence in darkness. In darkness one can not function effectively. So too, in inner darkness one can not function wisely. For example, you bang yourself with a chair in the dark and blame the chair for injuring you.

Similarly, in the inner darkness of one's soul, one is filled with desires and gets disappointed. The greatest mistake in life is not life but our foolishness. Life is a pilgrimage and desires are our inner death. The greatest calamity that has happened to life is that we are riding on the horse of desire, galloping to some destination, when we are in the world of God's love.

Reflect on this story.

A monk was travelling by train and carrying luggage on his head. The other passengers told him, 'You are so foolish, leave it on the ground.' He replied, 'Why burden the train? It is already loaded with so many of us.'

They said, 'Any way, the train alone takes the weight, so leave it on the floor of the train.'

The man kept the luggage down and started laughing. When asked why he was laughing, he said, 'You are also carrying the burden of worry on your head, any way the Lord alone is carrying that.'

Seek the Lord, seek Govinda.

VERSE 16

You are a nation within but who leads?

अग्रे वह्निः पृष्ठे भानुः
रात्रौ चुबुकसमर्पितजानुः ।
करतलभिक्षस्तरुतलवासः
तदपि न मुञ्चत्याशापाशः ।।
(भज-गोविन्दं... भज-गोविन्दं) (१६)

Agre Vahnih Prsthe Bhanuh
Ratrau Cubukasamarpitajanuh
Karatalabhiksastarutalavasah
Tadapi na muncatyasapasah
(Bhaja-Govindam Bhaja-Govindam...) (16)

अग्रे – in front, वह्निः – the fire, पृष्ठे – at the back, भानुः – the sun, रात्रौ – at night, चुबुक समर्पित जानुः – with (his) knees held to (his) chin (he sits), करतल भिक्ष – joining the palms to receive alms (he receives), तरुतलवासः – under the shelter of the tree (he lives), तदपि – and yet, न – never, मुञ्चति – spares (leaves) आशापाशः – noose of desires, भज – Seek, गोविन्दं – Govinda

In front of the fire, at the back the sun, late at night he sits with his knees held to his chin; he receives alms joining the palms and lives under the shelter of some tree and yet the noose of desire leaves him not! (Seek Govinda, seek Govinda).

'In front there is fire, at the back the sun, late at night he sits with his knees held to his chin; he receives alms in his own scooped palm and lives under the shelter of some tree and yet, the noose of desires spare him not.'

Seek Govinda seek Govinda.

This verse is attributed to Hastamalak, one of the disciples of Adi Shankaracharya.

In the previous verse the master's unfoldment depicted how typically the life a householder could be and how he is under the tyranny of desires and in this verse he depicts how even a monk has become a victim of desires.

In the Hindu tradition, an evil person is called as a *rakshasha* — a demon. The ancient text — *Puranas*, unfold how they are driven by evil desires; they were so destructive and a Divine force has to descend to destroy them. In a philosophical sense a demon is one who is not physically ugly but psychologically and spiritually ugly.

A mind driven by ignoble desires makes one ugly. One is destructive to himself and others. A Divine being is symbolically a Divine understanding. Such an understanding can destroy this demonic mind riddled by ignoble desires.

Now in a spiritual sense any desire is destructive, not only ignoble desires. First we have to drop ignoble desires and then at the next level even drop any desire. One has to understand what desire means in our tradition. A desire to 'become' happy is a desire that has to be dropped. But if one operates 'out of joy', a desire out of joy and not for joy, such a desire is not a problem in living.

Generally, people have a desire for name, fame, power, position, respectability and so on. Even a monk, so often is caught up in a desire to be respected and to be appreciated. Such desires are binding.

One cannot fight with desires. It is like fighting with darkness. When there is darkness you have to bring in light. Desire for joy is nothing but darkness. Bring in the light of joy... joy is here in this moment. This moment is full and complete and in such a space the desire to become happy will be dropped. You will have desires but that is 'out of joy and not for joy.'

The desire is a result of one's inner foolishness and not seeing the fullness of the moment. It is an ignorant part of oneself. So long as it exists, it does not matter whether one is a monk or a householder, the parade of foolishness continues.

Any desire that is 'for happiness' is insane including the desire for God or for enlightenment. Such desires drives one to the future and divorces one from the present. Life is always in the present; life is never in the future. Even the future shows up in the present.

The master unfolds that no matter however externally you are simple does not make a difference. 'In front the fire, at the back the sun, late at night he sits with his knees held to his chin; he receives alms in his own scooped-palm and lives under the shelter of some tree...'

One has to be inwardly simple. Externally one may be

simple, but if one is filled with desires, with rigidity, with seriousness, one's foolishness continues. It is like dressing a crocodile with a suite but still it remains a crocodile.

External change brings about really no change, inward change is the real change. Fill your mind with devotion, with sacredness. See this moment as sacred, discover the Divine and find joy dancing in the sunrise, sunset, in the birds chirping, and embrace life as a dance of ecstasy. In such a space desires drop.

One has to disarm oneself from desires. This personal disarmament is true non-violence. One may be externally non-violent but if one has desires, one is inwardly violent.

Your inner territory is like a nation within. Who is really governing this inner nation, devotion or desire? If a desire governs your inner territory, you have allowed a terrorist to rule your inner life.

So disarm this terrorist and transform him. This process of disarmament is the beginning of spirituality.

VERSE 17

How does knowledge of the world
differ from knowledge of the Self?

कुरुते गङ्गासागरगमनं
व्रतपरिपालनमथवा दानम् ।
ज्ञानविहीन: सर्वमतेन
भजति न मुक्तिं जन्मशतेन ॥
(भज-गोविन्दं... भज-गोविन्दं) (१७)

Kurute Gangasagaragamanam
Vrataparipalanamathava Danam
Jnanavihinah Sarvamatena
Bhajati Na Muktim Janmasatena
(Bhaja-Govindam Bhaja-Govindam...) (17)

कुरुते – goes to, गङ्गा सागर गमनं – to where the Ganges meets
the ocean, व्रतपरिपालनं – observes the vows, अथवा – or,
दानम् (कुरुते) – distributes gifts away, ज्ञान विहीन: – bereft of
spiritual realization, सर्वमतेन – according to all schools of
thought, भजति – (he) gains, न – not, मुक्तिं – liberation, जन्मशतेन
– even in hundred lives, भज – Seek, गोविन्दं – Govinda

One may go to where the Ganges meets the ocean, or observe the vows
or distribute gifts. If he is bereft of spiritual realisation according to
all schools of thought, he attains no liberation even in hundred lives.
(Seek Govinda, seek Govinda).

'One may on a pilgrimage to where the Ganges meets the ocean, called the *Gangasagar,* or observe vows or distribute gifts in charity. If he is devoid of true wisdom, according to all schools of thought, he gains no freedom even in a hundred lives.'

Seek Govinda seek Govinda.

This verse is attributed to Sri Subodha, one of the disciples of Adi Shankaracharya.

In the previous verse, *Hastamalak,* another disciple of Adi Shankaracharya denounced unintelligent practice of austerity by monks.

The Veda has two portions, the ritualistic portion — *karma kanda*, and the knowledge portion — *jnana kanda.* All ritualistic portions unfold discipline but that is not to be taken as be all and end all of the total understanding. When rituals are not backed with understanding and knowledge they become futile.

There is an essential practice and a secondary practise. The secondary practise like rituals equip one with discipline, faith, patience, detachment... that are essential for the purification of the mind but the real essential practice is true wisdom. Thus Subodha, one of the disciples of Adi Shankaracharya emphasises the need to focus on true knowledge.

There is knowledge of the world and knowledge of the Self. One acquires the knowledge of the world, but that does not provide true fulfillment. True knowledge is the knowledge of the Self and happiness exists in the Self.

Discover the hidden treasure within... is the invitation of the Master.

Everyone's life is filled with scriptures, the true wisdom of life. The outside world may contain reflections of life but they are only reflections. The moon reflected on the lake is not the real moon; it is called as *pratibimba nyaya*. Do not be deceived by such reflections. Search for the real moon, search for the real self.

Unless you discover the inner truth within yourself do not stop. Search for the truth. One will realise that in order to discover this truth, one should have enhanced a state of being. By devotion enhance your state of being, but search for the truth within you. It is not anywhere else but it is within you.

One who knows the self is not bound by the false. He will not be deceived by the reflections. In fact, he will rejoice the reflections, and hence he is not bound by it.

In fact, the ignorant, that happen to be the majority, are clouded by the egos. The ego is a substitute self and not the real Self. Hence the ego stands for — Edging God Out. As we are not aware of our true state, there is the presence of the ego. The absence of the true Self creates the presence of the false self.

So there is a false center and a true center in each one of us. The ignorant society supports the false center, which is nourished by greed for security, power, position, name, fame.... Thus, we are dominated by society and controlled by society. Due to this we fear society as society validates only this false center.

True knowledge is to stop playing with this toy called the ego and renounce it. By observing oneself, one finds that behind one's ego and behind one's thoughts, the true Self presides and resides.

'*Navadware Pure Dehi...*' the soul exists in this nine gated city called the body says the *Bhagavad Gita*.

Our true self is covered by the 'imaginary self' who creates the false personality called the ego. One has to notice how our imagination operates in our lives. We have to observe how it covers – *avaranam* and how it projects in our daily lives — *vikshepa*.

This false personality gives rise to many wrong emotional reactions. One has to observe and dis-identify from such emotions in order to gain true knowledge. False personality is based on pretence and tries to appease society, which supports the false center in oneself.

This false personality always wishes rewards, medals, seeks recognition and is crazy to be on the top. This is driven by vanity and inner foolishness. This is what Sri Subodha says, 'Devoid of knowledge — *jnana viheenaha*'.

The recognition of this game of delusion — *Maya*, based on imagination is a part of gaining true knowledge.

Reflect on this.

A man came to borrow a donkey from his neighbour.

'I have given it on loan', said the neighbour.

He.heard the donkey bray.

'But I hear the donkey bray', said the man.

'Who are you going to believe, the donkey or me?' retorted the neighbour.

So often we become more stupid than the donkey. Drop the ego and gain true knowledge.

VERSE 18

Renunciation — Is it a play of words or a possibility to live?

सुरमन्दिरतरुमूलनिवासः
शय्या भूतलमजिनं वासः ।
सर्वपरिग्रहभोगत्यागः
कस्य सुखं न करोति विरागः ॥
(भज-गोविन्दं... भज-गोविन्दं) (१८)

Suramandiratarumulanivasah
Sayya Bhutalamajinam Vasah
Sarvaparigrahabhogatyagah
Kasya Sukham Na Karoti Viragah
(Bhaja-Govindam Bhaja-Govindam...) (18)

सुर मन्दिर तरु मूल निवासः – residing in temples, under some trees, शय्या – bed (sleeping), भूतल – on the ground, अजिनं – (wearing) skin (deer's), वासः – cloth, सर्व परिग्रह – of the possession, भोगः – of thirst to enjoy, त्यागः – renouncing, कस्य – whose, सुखं – happiness, न – not, करोति – brings, विरागः – dispassion, भज – Seek, गोविन्दं – Govinda

Residing in temples, under some tree, sleeping on the bare ground, wearing a deer skin and thus renouncing all possessions and thirst to pleasure, to whom will not dispassion bring happiness? (Seek Govinda, seek Govinda).

'Sheltering in temples, under some tree, sleeping on the naked ground, wearing a deer-skin and thus renouncing all idea of possession and thirst to enjoy to whom will not dispassion — *vairagaya* bring happiness?'

This verse is attributed to Sureshwaracharaya, the disciple of the Adi Shankaracharya.

In the previous verse the unfoldment was on to denounce false detachment, but now Sureshwaracharaya invites us to the next level of how true detachment with knowledge will bring about happiness.

One cannot renounce the world. One can only renounce one's infatuation to the world. Wherever one goes there is a world, even if it is in the Himalayas, it is a part of the world, is it not?

So renouncing the world without understanding is foolishness, for world is present everywhere. But if you renounce your attachment and infatuation to the world, only then renunciation is a true renunciation.

In ancient Tibet there was a practice. A particular festival was celebrated by creating a *Yantra* — a mystical symbol in a temple. The whole monastery was involved. There was a complex calculation that went in to create this mystical symbol, the *yantra*. This would take many days. After creating the *yantra* and offering prayers, immediately the *yantra* would be wiped off.

It is created out of so much of care and wiping it off within few moments is a practice which symbolically represents that one should not be attached to anything.

Everything undergoes a change, so have the attitude of letting go.

In *yoga* practice after performing variety of *asanas or* yogic postures, one ends up with seeing the body as dead — *shavasana*, which is a form of relaxation. This is also with an understanding that the body will die at the end of one's life, thus sowing the value of detachment.

The world is not unreal but the way we see the world is unreal. Adi Shankaracharaya unfolds in many verses that the world is an illusion — *maya*. The world is an illusion but we see the world filled with attachment, infatuation and thus have an illusion of the perceived world. Detach from such a projected world.

We suffer not from the world but from our expectation of the world. Our mind is filled with likes and dislikes, with expectations and dogmas. If the world does not fit into our map of likes and dislikes we feel disappointed and hurt.

We blame the world for our sorrow. Without understanding we renounce the world but our foolish mind continues its illusion. It is like wearing a pair of dirty socks. Even if one goes to a clean place with dirty socks, it smells. It stinks not because one has visited newer places but because of one's socks.

Similarly, the world is not giving us unhappiness but our mind filled with likes and dislikes is giving us unhappiness. Such a mind when one renounces, one will be happy. 'Sheltering in temples, under some tree, sleeping on the naked ground, wearing a deer-skin and thus renouncing all ideas of possession and thirst to enjoy, to whom will not dispassion — *vairagya,* bring happiness.'

Work on such true detachment and not the foolish understanding of detachment.

Simplicity is not external but internal. With internal simplicity even with the most minimum possessions, one will be internally filled with happiness. Our expectations, likes and dislikes, dogmas make our mind complex. They create stress and sorrow in us.

To be contented with ourselves as we truly are, knowing the true Self is simplicity. In a state of deep sleep, when the complication of the mind is absent, are we happy or not? Where did the happiness come from? From within, is it not?

In the waking state our mind imposes a rule, a dogma. Driven by expectations our life revolves unwisely.

One needs to be simple, inwardly dropping expectations. It requires a special effort to just see life as it is and allowing one's inner self to guide. This is true simplicity. One need to trust that there is an intuitive power within oneself which guides one's life without desires.

Unfortunately, one's ego comes in the way and wants to be in charge and take control. This has to be recognized. By renouncing such a complex mind, one discovers true happiness that resides right in this moment.

To be detached means to be inwardly simple. In other words, it means living moment to moment with spontaneity and not according to one's ego, but according to one's inner being.

VERSE 19

The art of being in solitude and yet enjoying wordly pursuits

योगरतो वा भोगरतो वा
सङ्गरतो वा सङ्गविहीन: ।
यस्य ब्रह्मणि रमते चित्तं
नन्दति नन्दति नन्दत्येव ।।
(भज-गोविन्दं... भज-गोविन्दं) (१९)

Yogarato Va Bhogarato Va
Sangarato Va Sangavihinah
Yasya Brahmani Ramate Cittam
Nandati Nandati Nandatyeva
(Bhaja-Govindam Bhaja-Govindam...) (19)

योगरत: – (let) one who revels in Yoga, वा – or, भोगरत: – (let) one who revels in bhoga — pleasure, वा – or, सङ्गरत – (let) one seek enjoyment in company, वा – or, सङ्गविहीन: – (let) one who revels in aloneness away from the crowd, यस्य – for whom, ब्रह्मणि – in Brahman, रमते – revels (sports), चित्तं – the mind, नन्दति – (he) enjoys, नन्दति – (he) enjoys, नन्दत्येव – only he enjoys, भज – Seek, गोविन्दं – Govinda

Let one revel in yoga or let one revel in bhoga – pleasures. Let one seek joy in company or revel in aloneness. He, whose mind revels in Brahman, he enjoys... surely, he alone enjoys. (Seek Govinda, seek Govinda).

'Let one revel in *yoga* or let one revel in *bhoga*. Let one seek enjoyment in company or let one revel in solitude away from the crowd. He who's mind revels in Brahman, he enjoys... verily, he alone enjoys.'

Seek Govinda, seek Govinda.

This verse is attributed to Nityananda.

There is an outer world and there is an inner world. We focus on the outer world but what deeply impacts our lives are the inner world of thoughts and feelings. To change the inner world is most important. One can be outwardly in a comfortable domain but can still be comfortably miserable if one's mind is not at peace; peace not of a graveyard but peace of a rose garden. A mind at peace is a temple of bliss.

'Let one revel in *yoga* or let one revel in *bhoga*. Let one seek enjoyment in company or let one revel in solitude away from the crowd. He whose mind revels in Brahman, he enjoys... verily, he alone enjoys.'

The outer world is not important. The real focus should be in the inner world: one's inner state of mind and one's heart.

One has to learn to transform them. The mind is nothing but thoughts, and thoughts are expressions of memory. Our memory is stored in rolls, in different centers.

For example, it could be one's sex center, body center, emotional center and intellectual center. The external impressions fall on our centers. If one has disharmonized energies within, one's memory of these centers would be negative and such negative memories would make the mind restless.

In a restless state of mind 'Whether you are in *yoga* or *bhoga* — pleasurable enjoyment, whether you are in the company of the good or a recluse,' that will not make any difference. What will make a difference is a mind which is calm and reveling in the true joy of *Brahman*.

Brahman is not in time, it is eternity. It is indeed beyond time. Reveling in such a state of *Brahman* is nothing but reveling in timeless space. Time which is past, present and future prevents us from reaching a timeless state of *Brahman* which is a higher state. Man has to be twice born — *dvija*, out of time and space in order for his mind to be enlightened and to attain enlightenment — *nirvana*.

A mind bathed by such an understanding of timelessness will not be a victim of external situations of life or else the mind would be living in the past.

We do not live in the world. We live in our minds and our minds are reliving in our past. So our present is nothing but an extension of the past. In such a mind one cannot see anything new, neither one can see the timeless *Brahman*.

Think in a new way, learn to experience timelessness. We live in the 'Time Body' and there is a timeless presence also. Time is an expression of thought and between the thoughts there is thoughtlessness which is timelessness. Enter into the gap between thoughts and see a state beyond the mind. This will truly liberate you. Seek Govinda, seek Govinda.

Reflect on this.

A student: 'Why do we suffer?'

Master: All our suffering comes from wrong programming. Do not blame the world. Change your inner programming of the mind. It is the machinery inside you which is wrongly set. Change it and you will see suffering is an illusion, a dream.'

VERSE 20

Ways to face and encounter death

भगवद्गीता किञ्चिदधिता
गङ्गा जललवकणिका पीता ।
सकृदपि येन मुरारिसमर्चा
क्रियते तस्य यमेन न चर्चा ।।
(भज-गोविन्दं... भज-गोविन्दं) (२०)

Bhagavadgita Kincidadhita
Ganga Jalalavakanika Pita
Sakrdapi Yena Murarisamarca
Kriyate Tasya Yamena Na Carca
(Bhaja-Govindam Bhaja-Govindam...) (20)

भगवद् गीता – The Bhagavad Gita, किञ्चित् – (even) a little, अधिता – has studied, गङ्गा जल लव कणिका – a drop of Ganges water, पीता – has sipped, सकृत् अपि – at least once, येन – by whom, मुरारिसमर्चा – worship of the Lord Murali, (मुरस्य अरि: – the enemy of mura, a raksasa), क्रियते – is done, तस्य – to him, यमेन – with Yama, the Lord of Death, न – never, चर्चा – quarrel (conversation) भज – Seek, गोविन्दं – Govinda

To one who has studied the Bhagavad Gita even a little, who has sipped at least a drop of Ganges water, who has worshipped at least once Lord Murari, there is no conversation (quarrel) with Yama, the Lord of Death. (Seek Govinda, seek Govinda).

'To one who has studied the *Bhagavad Gita*, even a little, who has sipped at least a drop of the Ganges water, who has worshipped at least once Lord Murari; to Him there is no discussion (quarrel) with Yama, the Lord of death.'

Seek Govinda, seek Govinda.

This verse is attributed to Sri Anandagiri, another disciple of Adi Shankaracharya.

Vedas are the oldest spiritual literature in the world. There are four Vedas. The essence of the Veda is freedom of the soul — *moksha*. The *Bhagavad Gita* is the essence of the Veda. It is in the *Bheeshma Parva* of the *Mahabharata*. When Arjuna had a breakdown in the battle-field as he was to fight his own *gurus* and cousins, Lord Krishna unfolds the *Bhagavad Gita*.

The Lord helps to convert a breakdown into a breakthrough, transforms worry into wisdom, frustration into fascination. If this can happen right in the battlefield to Arjuna, it can happen to anyone, whoever can even practice a little of the *Bhagavad Gita*.

The essence of the *Bhagavad Gita* is that whatever be the situation — *parisithiti*, one has to change the state of the mind — *manostithi* and then change the state of *being* — *atmastiti*. This is the path of transformation. The teaching helps us to change the state of mind and state of *being*. Then one will not be a victim to a situation. More than the situation it is the state of the mind and *being* which impact our lives.

In the *Mahabharata*, Vidura – the prime minister of

Hastinapur tells Kunti — the mother of the Pandavas that Karna – a close aide of Dhuryodhana and King of Ang is whipping himself by saying that he is a son of a charioteer — *suta putra* and not a warrior — *kshatriya* and thus the situation in his life was the source of his misery.

But look at me says Vidura, 'I am the son of a servant — *dasi putra*. Even though I am the prime minister of Hastinapur and the brother of King Dritharastra I do not whip myself saying I am a son of a servant.' As far as Vidhura was concerned, it was not the situation but the state of his mind and *being* that really enlivened his life.

If one can even grasp a little of the *Bhagavad Gita,* one's life will change. The Lord says, 'Lift yourself by yourself, do not condemn yourself, for you are your friend and you are your enemy.'

'Who has sipped at least a drop of the Ganges water, who has worshipped at least once Lord Murari, to Him there is no discussion (quarrel) with Yama, the Lord of death.'

The Ganges flows from the head of Lord Shiva and so it is symbolic that it is the river of knowledge. So taking a dip in true knowledge liberates one. We live in the world of 'personality' which leads us to bondage — *samsara,* a world of deficiency. To drop 'personality' and to operate out of 'essence' is the core teaching. 'Essence' leads us to inner sufficiency or inner freedom — *nirvana.*

Personality comes from 'persona': mask. In Greek plays and dramas, one wear masks and dance. Similarly, we wear psychological masks and do not see our true nature, our inner 'essence'. Learning to drop one's inner mask and see oneself is the essence of true knowledge.

'Who has worshipped at least once Lord Murari; to Him there is no discussion (quarrel) with Yama, the Lord of death.'

Lord Murari stands for the waves of bliss, love and beauty — *ananda lahari, prema lahari* and *soundarya lahari*. Lord Murari is a 'state of being', a state of 'awakened consciousness'. To worship the Lord is to live and revel in that state of *being* and to live that awakened consciousness.

If one has experienced living in the states of love and bliss —*prema lahari* and *ananda lahari*, the Lord of Death will not touch such a person untimely. The Lord of Death is nothing but a dead state of consciousness where one has not seen the richness and aliveness of life. People are living a dead life and not a life of ecstasy.

Once you live a life of ecstasy or 'Krishna consciousness' how can death happen? Death to — life which indeed is bliss...

For a devotee even death comes dancing. Every moment he rejoices. He sees beauty in *what is* and not *what should be*. Blissfulness is our inner nature that we have to claim. That is why in deep sleep without effort and without any object one is happy.

Bliss is the nature of one's inner self. We cannot manufacture it. We can allow it to happen but we can not produce it. We can block it from happening like we can block the sun rays from entering our room. Blocking it is by one's ego and a non-spiritual life.

Once we have tasted the discipline of being blissful and not allowing the ego to interfere, death cannot happen. Death here is not physical death but a psychological death.

VERSE 21

What is law of grace and how does one experience it?

पुनरपि जननं पुनरपि मरणं
पनरपि जननीजठरे शयनम् ।
इह संसारे बहुदुस्तारे
कृपयाऽपारे पाहि मुरारे ।।
(भज-गोविन्दं... भज-गोविन्दं) (२१)

Punarapi jananijathare Sayanam
Iha Samsare Bahudustare
Krpayapare Pahi Murare
(Bhaja-Govindam Bhaja-Govindam...) (21)

पुनः अपि – once again, जननं – birth, पुनः अपि – once again,
मरणं – death, पुनरपि – (and) again, जननीजठरे – in the mother's
womb, शयनम् – lying, इह – here, संसारे – in this (samsara), बहु
दुस्तारे – which is very hard to cross over, अपारे – (samsara)
which has no end, कृपया – through thy infinite kindness,
पाहि – save, मुरारे – Oh, destroyer of Mura, भज – Seek, गोविन्दं –
Govinda

*Taking birth and death and again lying in mother's womb – this
samsara – worldly life is very hard to cross over. Through thy infinite
kindness Save Me Oh, destroyer of Mura. (Seek Govinda, seek
Govinda).*

'Again birth, again death, again reborn in mother's womb — this *samsara* process is very hard to cross over….. Save Me, Murari through thy infinite kindness.'

Seek Govinda, seek Govinda.

More often people's life has been a journey from one state of deficiency to another state of deficiency. We are born with inner fullness but we go on losing it by searching outside ourselves. One needs food, shelter, clothing and many more essentials but if one's whole life is spent only on those basic needs, it is a foolish living. We are not open to see within ourselves and hence we lose this experience of inner fullness.

The world can give us pleasures in life but what we are searching is bliss. Our search is like an old lady searching under the street light for a needle that she had dropped in her hut, and her hut was not lit.

A foolish person is one who has wasted his lifetime by being too extrovert and has stopped learning the art of seeking within. His seeking outside has become destructive as he is destroying the very planet out of greed to be happy and joyous.

The way to enlightenment, to inner freedom, to inner joy is to be unidentified with the body and mind phenomena. But we know ourselves only as the body, mind and its emotions. Our identity is so shallow that we fail to see that we have a body and a mind but that we are not just the body and the mind. For example, I have a car, this is different from I am the car. I am the body is different from I have a body. This knowledge is not deep rooted in many and thus one is caught in the cycle of birth and death.

Birth and death is a search for fullness and this search is painful for the one who is searching if one is drunk with ignorance and goes about misunderstanding life. Deep within, one knows something is wrong and experiences misery.

It is like a drunken man recognizing his house. When he tries to open the door he feels the house is moving and shaking and he is angry with himself as to why the house is moving. He fails to realise that it is due to his state of drunkenness.

One has to remember constantly that 'I am not the body but I have the body, I am not the mind but I have a mind.' Slowly distancing from the body, one will dis-identify from body consciousness and become soul consciousness.

One has to go on witnessing one's body and mind. When such witnessing experience deepens, one is on the verge of a break-through. Then all of a sudden all boundaries would vanish and one's experience would be a state of infinite — *aham brahmasmi*.

For such an experience to occur, one's negative mind and negative emotions have to be transformed. These negativities create a world of misery. Understand that if one is miserable, it is the working of one's negative mind and its emotions.

To be miserable is an unnatural state. To be blissful is a natural state. Thus effortlessly in sleep one is blissful. One is unconscious of this truth and this unconsciousness makes one identify with one's shadow, the body and mind. To be conscious of one's unconscious is a part of true spiritual living.

Meditation and spiritual life are simply waking up to this reality. The *Veda* says, 'Get up and wake up.'

Being spiritual means you have decided not to be in an unconscious state. The commitment is to be conscious but the power of unconscious is pulling you. This struggle has taken many births.

'Save me, Murari through thy infinite kindness.'

Science discovered the law of gravitation and religion operates on the law of grace. The great masters meditated and discovered their energies moving upwards and thus tuned to the law of grace which is higher than the many laws operating the world.

When one lives a loving life, a life filled with love, seeing life as an expression of God, in such a space there is grace and through grace one reaches God. So from love to grace to God is the Divine way.

Grace descends onto a pure person. In fact, grace is always present but one's inner instrument of mind and heart should be able to receive the fine vibrations of God's kindness in the form of grace. Thus seek Govinda, seek Govinda.

VERSE 22

Preparation for wise living to realise the ultimate truth

रथ्याचर्पटविरचितकन्थ:
पुण्यापुण्यविवर्जितपन्थ: ।
योगी योगनियोजितचित्तो
रमते बालोन्मत्तवदेव ।।
(भज-गोविन्दं... भज-गोविन्दं) (२२)

Rathyacarpataviracitakanthah
Punyapunyavivarjitapanthah
Yogi Yoganiyojitacitto
Ramate Balonmattavadeva
(Bhaja-Govindam Bhaja-Govindam...) (22)

रथ्या – the road, चर्पट – rags/old cloth, विरचित – made of, कन्थ: – cloth, पुण्य-अपुण्य – merit and demerit, विवर्जित – well left, पन्थ: – the path, योगी – the yogin (sage), योगनियोजित चित्त: – whose understanding mind is joined in perfect yoga, रमते – sports (lives there after), बालवत् एव – as a child (or), उन्मत्तवत् एव – as a madman, भज – Seek, गोविन्दं – Govinda

The yogin who wears only rags made of old cloth, who walks the path that is beyond merit and demerit, whose understanding mind is joined in perfect yoga with its goal, revels (in truth) and lives thereafter — as a child or as a madman. (Seek Govinda, seek Govinda).

'The yogin who wears nothing but just rags made of old cloth, rejected by others, picked up from the streets and stitched together, who walks the path that is beyond merit and demerit, whose mind is joined in perfect Yoga with a goal, he revels in God-Consciousness and lives thereafter as a child or as a madman.'

An enlightened person having gained Divine wisdom drops his individuality. Such a person will be viewed by others as a madman or as a child. The ignorant is considered more of a social being. He is a part of society. He is either controlled consciously or unconsciously by society. Thus many are caught up in 'looking good.' Many sacrifice 'feeling good' and 'being good' for the sake of 'looking good.' Why is it so? It is because one is a social being and controlled by social expectations.

If one is on the path of a spiritual journey, one is more focused on 'being good' and does not unwisely dance to people's expectation. In fact, society views such a person as a mad man.

Such a person lives innocently like a child or termed as a madman from others point of view. People cannot understand that such a state of one's *being* is of that where one experiences oneness.

A wise man is like a King of the inner world. He may be a beggar outwardly but feels like a King inwardly. It is a tradition in India where even a King used to touch the feet of a monk recognizing that the monk is a King inside. True Kingdom is the Kingdom of the soul. A monk may outwardly look like a beggar.

Reflect on this story.

There was a monk leading a simple and spontaneous life. The people in the town respected his simplicity as it was well within their yardstick of a definition of a wise person. In the town a young unwed woman became pregnant which was an embarrassment. In order to save her boyfriend she declared to the elders of the town that this monk was responsible for her pregnancy.

The monk when encountered only answered, 'Is that so?' He was shunted out of the town with the pregnant woman.

The monk went along with the pregnant women, but did not make her wrong for her untruth utterance and the shame that she brought upon the monk. He continued to beg in the neighbouring village not only for himself but for the pregnant woman who sullied his character.

After a few days the woman felt guilty, realised her folly, went back to her town, and revealed the truth of who really was responsible for her pregnancy. The elders of the town who banished the monk were repenting for humiliating the monk. They came in scores and profusely apologized. The monk only answered, 'Is that so?'

A wise person has no image, thus is inwardly free. In such a case he will be viewed as a child without any internal image as he is free. Such an inner freedom is unheard of by the ignorant. But the ignorant is guided, controlled, and bound by their image.

A wise person is in perfect yoga as he is not a slave to anything, he is inwardly free. He does not wear masks to impress others. He is one who has won over the unconsciousness in him. A King outwardly has his unconsciousness and so he is a slave to power, money... and goes about pretending to be powerful.

But a true King is a yogi who is inwardly free even though externally he may look like a beggar or a mad man. He has wisdom which is just not like a dry knowledge. Only his wisdom is not recongnised and understood by others and so often he is treated as a mad person.

'The one is beyond merit and demerit.'

Even the desire to gain merit is a subtle bondage. The fear of avoiding demerit is also a subtle bondage. The greed to be somebody and the fear of being nobody is a great bondage. A yogi has no greed and no fear.

Quite often we find people who are confused in their lives as they are victims to their greed and fear. They create psychological rigidities and do not flow and dance like a child. A dance reaches the peak when the dancer disappears and only the dance remains. The art of dissolving is a great art.

If one is wise, one sees the futility of greed and fear. Greed and fear prepares one to live life as though without them it is impossible to live. Most of us are preparing to live life but hardly living life. Greed is like declaring inside you to postpone your life for tomorrow. People are used to living a life of greed and fear as they have not yet discovered themselves as *deathless* beings.

Greed and fear happens because one is afraid to die, afraid to face death. One hankers after more money and more power because one knows death is somewhere round the corner waiting and one may have fear of losing everything at once. But a wise person discovers that he is a *deathless* being and thus inwardly free.

To really grow up is to see oneself in a state of '*deathlessness.*' Such a person is externally like a 'child or a madman.'

Reflect on this Zen story.

'One second please!' said a fish in the ocean to the older fish.

'You are older and wiser than me. Where can I find the ocean which people talk of, they say it is a vast span of water all over?'

'You are in the ocean,' said the older fish.

'No, this is water but I am looking for the ocean,' said the young fish and went away disappointed with the answer.

'Whose mind is joined in perfect yoga with its goal?'

A mind without an ego reveals in yoga. Ego divides and thus one feels it is other than oneself. Once you feel that the other is different, you are in conflict with the other. Such a life leads to inner pain and stress. A wise person knows he is not different essentially than the other.

In Vedanta it is said a space in the pot feels limited by the pot and feels other than the outer space. But in reality the pot exists in space. The space in the pot is the same as the space outside the pot. It is an illusion that space is limited by the pot but appears it is limited. Similarly, the nature of consciousness in the body is same outside the body also. It is a matter of one's focus that requires change.

So the consciousness is not limited by the body or ego and thus it is full and complete by itself. A yogi is one who is anchored in such fullness and reveals in perfect yoga. A wise person's focus is so clear that he is inwardly free.

'A wise person is beyond merit and demerit.'

Only ego has merit and demerit. A wise person is beyond ego and revels in God consciousness.

VERSE 23

Experiencing inwardly is liberating

कस्त्वं कोऽहं कुत आयातः
का मे जननी को मे तातः ।
इति परिभावय सर्वमसारं
विश्वं त्यक्त्वा स्वप्नविचारम् ॥
(भज-गोविन्दं... भज-गोविन्दं) (२३)

Kastvam Koham Kuta Ayatah
Ka Me Janani Ko Me Tatah
Iti Paribhavaya Sarvamasaram
Visvam Tyaktva Svapnavicaram
(Bhaja-Govindam Bhaja-Govindam...) (23)

कः – who, त्वम् – (are) you, कः – who, अहम् – am I, कुतः – from where, आयातः – did I come, का – who(is), मे – my, जननी – mother, कः – who (is), मे तातः – my father, इति – thus, परिभावय – reflect, सर्व – all, असारं – essenceless, विश्वं – the entire world of experience, त्यक्त्वा – leaving aside, स्वप्नविचारम् – a mere dream, भज – Seek, गोविन्दं – Govinda

Who are you? Who am I? From where did I come? Who is my mother? Who is my father? Thus reflect, leaving aside the entire world, essence-less and a mere dream born out of imagination. (Seek Govinda, seek Govinda).

'Who are you? Who am I? From where did I come? Who is my mother? Who is my father? Thus enquire, leaving aside the entire world of experiences — *vishwam*, essence-less and a mere dreamland, born of imagination.'

Seek Govinda, seek Govinda.

This verse is attributed to Sri Yogananda, another disciple of Adi Shankaracharya.

Along the line most of us have stopped searching within. The path of spirituality is a search for the miraculous. Most of us conclude and such conclusion becomes the basis of our thinking or feeling. We are not internally free to search. If one pauses, one can come in touch with the fact that we are all seeking for the miraculous.

There are schools of spirituality focused only on morality. There are schools which demand you to renounce the world and live in monastery. But the teaching of Adi Shankaracharya is to make us look within and ask the basic questions that we have taken for granted.

We take for granted who we are. Not knowing who we are, we ourselves have become a prisoner. So wherever we go we create our own prison, like a spider creating its own cobweb wherever it goes.

One may say, 'I am a father or a husband.' With reference to your son you are a father, with reference to your wife you are a husband, with reference to your student you are a teacher, with reference to your father you are a son... But these are references but with reference to yourself, who are you? Search inwardly not intellectually but existentially.

Experiencing yourself inwardly would be liberating.

We are lost in our personality which is a persona — a cover, a face. Hence, Zen masters tell us to see our original face, other than the mask, other than the personality, other than the roles we play. There is 'essence' in us. This 'essence' is our *being*. This 'essence' is like space and without space there cannot be a room. One has to discover one's inner space or inner essence.

Our personality, our ego is the barrier that blocks our contact with our true nature, our true essence. One has to enquire and dis-identify with the changing to discover the changeless. This changeless 'I' is the basis of our thoughts and feelings. Thoughts and feelings do come and go, but the changeless space is the real 'Me', the real core, the real center.

'Who is my mother, who is my father?'

Father and mother are the roles that one plays but the essence is other than the roles. Search for it, not philosophically but through true enquiry.

'Thus enquire leaving aside the entire world of experiences, essence-less and a mere dreamland born out of imagination.'

Reflect on this.

꙰ 'If you make me your authority and refuse to see, you harm yourself because you refuse to see things for yourself,' said the master.

And after some time the master continued, 'You harm me too because you refuse to see me as I am and so you think, my son.'

Our experience of the world is a dreamland as we see what we *want to see* rather than see *what is*. The world is unreal in the sense that we project on the world our expectations, and conclusions.

Thus we do not see *what is* as *what is*. It is like a hungry man who looks at the moon and sees it as a piece of cheese. We do not see God's world, but we see our subjective world born out of our likes and dislikes. Thus, the master is inviting us to enquire and look within.

VERSE 24

Equal minded in all circumstances — Is it a myth or a reality?

त्वयि मयि चान्यत्रैको विष्णुः
व्यर्थ कुप्यसि मय्यसहिष्णुः ।।
भव समचित्तः सर्वत्र त्वं
वाञ्छस्यचिराद्यदि विष्णुत्वम् ।।
(भज-गोविन्दं... भज-गोविन्दं) (२४)

Tvayi Mayi Canyatraiko Visnuh
Vyartham Kupyasi Mayyasahisnuh
Bhava Samacittah Sarvatra tvam
Vanchasyaciradyadi Visnutvam
(Bhaja-Govindam Bhaja-Govindam...) (24)

त्वयि – in you, मयि – in me, च – and, अन्यत्र – in all other places, (too), एकः – but one, विष्णुः – all pervading reality (Visnu), व्यर्थ – unnecessarily, कुप्यसि – you are getting angry, मयि – with me, असहिष्णुः – being impatient, भव – become, समचित्त – equal-minded, सर्वत्र – everywhere (in all circumstances), त्वं – you, वाञ्छसि यदि – if you want, अचिरात् – soon, विष्णुत्वं – the Visnu – Status, भज – Seek, गोविन्दं – Govinda

In you, in me and in other places too there is but one all pervading reality. Being impatient, you are unnecessarily getting angry with me. If you want to attain enlightenment (Vishnutvam), be equal minded in all circumstances. (Seek Govinda, seek Govinda).

'In you, in me and in (all) other places too, there is but one all-pervading reality Vishnu. Being impatient, you are unnecessarily getting angry with me. If you want to attain soon the Vishnu-status, be equal indeed in all the circumstances.'

Seek Govinda, seek Govinda.

This verse is attributed to Vishnutwam, another disciple of Adi Shankaracharya.

There are various facets in each one of us. For example, there is a superficial '*me*' and there is an essential '*me*.' There is a social '*me*' and there is a spiritual '*me*.' There is a circumference and there is a center.

We are lost in the circumference, in the superficial, in the social world and hence miss the essential. The whole search of a spiritual person is searching for this essential '*me*.'

We are, by default due to ignorance, lost in the unessential and thus miss the essential.

The center in oneself, the core of oneself is all pervading. If this oneness is seen all around, the differences will not create chaos. For example, the body has eyes, ears, nose, hands, legs... and each function differently, each look differently but the total individual is one. Please do not miss seeing this important dimension of oneness.

It is like the phenomenon of electricity which is one entity called as energy but it manifests in a bulb, in a fan, in a refrigerator differently, but the source is one entity of electrical energy. Similarly, the waves in the ocean appear differently, in size, in power but the water is the essence. The soul in all of us is one reality.

It appears as if there is duality in form and shape. If such duality is perceived in life with misunderstanding, one is bound to be in illusion. But if one sees non-duality in all of them, one sees the reality of *Vishnutwam*.

For example, love is the essential emotion and jealousy is the unessential emotion. If one is anchored in jealousy, one loves to criticise others, loves to find fault in others. There is a feeling of superiority over the others. This is falsehood.

One has to observe the play of unessential emotions in life and slowly discard and renounce it as it would not help in the quality of one's life. When unessential emotions and unessential thoughts parade in our lives, we become impatient, we become angry and thus we do not see the 'all pervading reality — *Vishnu.*'

'Being impatient, you are unnecessarily getting angry with me',

So in other words, the master is inviting us to drop the non-essential emotions. If a mirror is dusty it reflects but without clarity. Similarly, if the mind is filled with impurity or impatience, the truth will not be cognized.

Whenever an impulse falls on the mind it falls in one's memory. If a person is not in the practice of spiritual discipline, such impulses could show up as negative memory. A negative memory would connect to other negative memories of the past and thus unhappy and negative memories network occurs in one's mind. A chain of such negative memories makes one impatient.

'Drop this impatience', says the máster and invites us to see all external impulses fall in happy and positive memories. A spiritual person looks at a difficulty as God's method to teach one to be tolerant. Every difficulty therefore, becomes an opportunity to grow. Hence, the master says, 'Do not get angry and be impatient.'

'Learn to be in a state of equal minded in all circumstances.'

This is possible when we learn from difficult situations. If one starts treating difficulty as a Divine method, it helps to teach oneself so that one can grow.

Every drunkard should teach us that drinking is bad habit, so do not be upset with a drunkard. Learn and grow from every situation. Learn the right lessons from life. That is possible if one is calm and evenminded. 'That is the way and this is the path... even mindedness.'

Start to think in a new way. Do not get hooked to your way of looking at life.

Once you are on this path, unwrapped gifts in your understanding would open up. Life would have a different poetry. It is not going to be only prose. You will be able to listen to the music and the mystery of life which is beyond your gross logic.

A master told his student:

'The words of what I say appear ordinary but the meaning is extraordinary.'

'How to get the extraordinary meaning from these ordinary words,' asked the student?

'Whenever I make a statement, shake it so well where the words drop and let the meaning light your heart. Then you will realise the extraordinary meaning from my ordinary words,' replied the master.

VERSE 25

Self remembering and purification of love

शत्रौ मित्रे पुत्रे बन्धौ
मा कुरु यत्नं विग्रहसन्धौ !
सर्वस्मिन्नपि पश्यात्मानं
सर्वत्रोत्सृज भेदज्ञानम् ।।
(भज-गोविन्दं... भज-गोविन्दं) (२५)

Satrau Mitre Putre Bandhau
Ma Kuru Yatnam Vigrahasandhau
Sarvasminnapi Pasyatmanam
Sarvatrotsrja Bhedajnanam
(Bhaja-Govindam Bhaja-Govindam...) (25)

शत्रौ – against an enemy, मित्रे – against a friend, पुत्रे – against a son, बन्धौ – against a relative, मा – never, कुरु – do, यत्नं – strive, विग्रहसन्धौ – for fighting and reconciliation, सर्वस्मिन् अपि – in everything (everywhere), पश्य – see, आत्मानं – the Self, सर्वत्र – everywhere, उत्सृज – pluck & throw away, भेदज्ञानम् – the sense of difference (born out of ignorance), भज – Seek, गोविन्दं – Govinda

Strive not, waste not your energy to fight against an enemy or make friends with your enemy, son or relative. Seeing the Self everywhere, pluck and throw away differences born out of ignorance. (Seek Govinda, seek Govinda).

'Strive not; waste not your energy to fight against, or to make friends, with your enemy, friend, son or relative. Seeking the Self everywhere, lift the sense of differences, that is born out of ignorance.'

Seek Govinda, seek Govinda.

One has to be aware whether one's psychological energy is being sapped. A mind which is anxious is a worried mind whose energy dissipates and such a mind can never see oneness.

Reflect on this story that I came across.

A student went to a Zen master and requested him to teach him. The master asked him to take a bucket and fetch water from the well and fill a nearby tank.

The student tried to draw water from the well but found only an empty bucket coming up. His effort went on for quite sometime, and the student finally gave up his effort and confessed his inability to fulfil the master's directive.

The master made him see that the bucket had many holes and those holes were responsible for emptying the water out of the bucket.

Similarly, if one's mind is filled with holes of worry and being upset, it prevents oneself from filling one's *being* with truth.

One has to stop one's psychological energy from being sapped. One has to understand that there are two aspects present in oneself. There is a domain of knowledge that one possess and there is the domain of *being* that one is endowed with. One's knowledge has to impact one's *being* or else it will be like a load of sandalwood on a donkey's back.

If one observes oneself closely, one finds whenever one identifies or gets attached to something, there is bound to be sapping of one's psychological energy. Non-identification is an important discipline. Not being attached is a wonderful discipline.

Is it not natural for us to be attached to the one whom we love?

Love has to go through purification. It is like there is a good father and not a loving father, a good mother and not a wise mother. Similarly, love when purified would show up as a concern for the other but not when one is worried and attached.

In such an understanding one would be caring and not attached. Thus, one is not identified to the loved ones. The more one practices 'non-consideration,' or not worrying, there will be very little chance of sapping of energy. Therefore, one has to 'self-remember' the teaching of the enlightened masters as:

• Non-identification

• Non-consideration

• Self-remembering

• Knowledge of being

When knowledge of being takes place, one sees the Self

everywhere and the differences or duality would be just an illusion.

It is similar to a movie screen. It is an illusion but appears real. One sees non-duality in spite of duality.

Reflect deeply on this point.

Continuing further,

VERSE 26

Knowledge of self is indeed knowledge of joy

कामं क्रोधं लोभं मोहं
त्यक्त्वाऽत्मानं पश्यति सोऽहम् ।
आत्मज्ञान-विहीना मूढा –
स्ते पच्यन्ते नरकनिगूढा: ।।
(भज-गोविन्दं... भज-गोविन्दं) (२६)

Kamam Krodham Lobham Moham
Tyaktvatmanam Pasyati Soham
Atmajnana Vihina Mudha
Ste Pacyante Narakanigudhah
(Bhaja-Govindam Bhaja-Govindam...) (26)

कामं – desire, क्रोधं – anger, लोभं – greed, मोहं – delusion, त्यक्त्वा – having renounced, आत्मानं – the self, पश्यति – see (the seeker), स: अहम् – he am I, आत्मज्ञान-विहीना: – those who have no Self knowledge, मूढा: – the fools, ते – they, पच्यन्ते – are tortured, नरक-निगूढा: – in hell as captives, भज – Seek, गोविन्दं – Govinda

Having renounced anger, greed and delusion the seeker sees in the self, "He am I". They are fools who have no self-knowledge and they as captives in hell are tortured. (Seek Govinda, seek Govinda).

'Leaving desire, anger, greed and delusion, the seeker sees in the self, 'He am I.' they are fools who have no self-knowledge and they as captives in hell are tortured.'

Seek Govinda, seek Govinda.

There are two types of desires. They are desire 'to *become*' and the desire '*to do.*' The desire to become is the problem which pulls one into the world of deficiency. 'I want this or that to become happy' means silently one declares within oneself that 'I am unhappy now and by achieving this goal I am going to become happy.' Thus, the happiness is in the world outside but the trut is that happiness is within. For example, in a state of deep sleep one is happy without objects or without any achievements.

So happiness is experienced from within.

Whereas, 'desire to do' does not pose a problem. The question is – are one's actions coming out of happiness or for happiness? This is the primary question that one has to revel in.

Desire is insane only if one is living for the future and missing the present. Time is past, present and future, but life shows up in the present. Treating this very moment as a present is living in the present. One's desires should not drive one away from the present. So the master is lovingly telling us to drop such desires that makes one live in the future.

Anger happens when one's desire is obstructed in fulfilling it. It happens as an obstruction in fulfilling one's desires and results in pain. Anger is bondage. It blocks one's free flow of joy.

Seen from another angle, anger is active sadness and sadness is passive anger. Whenever one is angry one is sad within. Drop one's sadness. Discover, 'I am that joy' and sadness and anger would drop by themselves.

The 'knowledge of the Self' is the answer to most of our problems. The knowledge of the Self is knowledge of joy. We are 'captives in hell' as we are not experiencing joy in the *here* and *now*.

As we are not experiencing joy, we have become a victim of 'greed.' The greed to become somebody and the fear of being nobody is the greatest fear that we undergo. We have to see this truth in our daily lives.

Reflect on this incident.

'What are you searching for dear lady,' asked a young man seeing an old woman searching under a streetlight.

'I am searching for my keys,' answered the old woman.

'Where did you drop it,' asked the young man.

'In my hut,' she replied.

'But why are you searching under the streetlight here?'

'Because there is no electricity in my hut,' replied the old woman.

Search for God. Search for joy within. Searching for joy where it is not, is like the old woman searching for her keys under the streetlight.

VERSE 27

Is society's collective context and environment impact affecting you?

गेयं गीतनामसहस्रं
ध्येयं श्रीपतिरूपमजस्रम् ।
नेयं सज्जनसङ्गे चित्तं
देयं दीनजनाय च वित्तम् ॥
(भज-गोविन्दं... भज-गोविन्दं) (२७)

Geyam Gitanamasahasram
Dhyeyam Sripatirupamajasram
Neyam Sajjanasange Cittam
Deyam Dinajanaya Ca Vittam
(Bhaja-Govindam Bhaja-Govindam...) (27)

गेयं – worthy of being (sung) गीता – Bhagavad Gita, नामसहस्रम् – Sahasranamam, ध्येयं – is to be meditated upon, श्रीपति रूपं – the form of the Lord of Lakshmi, जस्रम् – always, नेयं – (the mind) is to be led, सज्जन-सङ्गे – in the association (company) of the good, चित्तं – the mind, देयं – is to be given, दीनजनाय च – to the needy, वित्तम् – wealth, भज – Seek, गोविन्दं – Govinda

The Bhagavad Gita and Sahasranama are worthy to be sung; always the form of Lord of Lakshmi is to be meditated upon; the mind is to be led towards the company of the good; wealth is to be given to the needy. (Seek Govinda, seek Govinda).

'*Bhagavad Gita* and *Vishnu Sahasranama* are to be chanted, always the form of the Lord of Lakshmi is to be meditated upon; the mind is to be led towards the company of the good; wealth is to disturbed to the needy.'

This is the concluding verse of the 14th disciple of Adi Shankaracharya on his way to Kashi yatra. Reading *Bhagavad Gita* & *Vishnu Shahasranama* and meditating on the form of the *Lord Vishnu* is a part of giving conscious pause and direction.

To give oneself a conscious pause, a conscious shock and a conscious direction is the very need in one's spiritual path. One needs to give a pause and observe oneself in a state of awareness. Is one's knowledge encompassed only in the intellectual domain? One has to travel through the three domains called *thinking to feeling to being.*

Whatever one's knowledge be, it should result in one's change of one's feeling. For example, to be in a loving state is just a thought. But the question is — has that thought changed one's feeling? From such a feeling does one's *being* show up in a loving space? This has to be observed and discovered through a conscious pause.

'Conscious shock' is to be administered upon oneself when one is stuck to one's thinking and not transforming to one's feeling and being. At that point it is the right to give a shock to one-self consciously.

Chanting of the *Sahasranama* of Lord Vishnu will help in changing the feeling consciously. There are many practices in the Hindu tradition that provide shocks to one's mechanical centres to help them move towards magnetic centres.

'Conscious direction' is something which we need to remember always. Conscious direction is based on the teachings of enlightened masters to re-orient ourselves. Thus reading the *Bhagavad Gita* will lead us on a right path towards transformation.

In everyone's life there is an 'environmental impact' and an 'experiential impact.' One should be consciously exposed to an 'educational impact' also which is based on a conscious pause, a conscious shock and a conscious direction.

If we look closely, today's society context is not transformation. It is money, power, name, fame, pride... on which society respects an individual. They start unconsciously impacting and polluting a context of transformation of an individual. Thus, it can be termed as an 'environmental impact.'

One needs to be aware of this fact and not get unduly influenced by society. It is also true that our own experiences at times pollute us. Sometimes, one starts doubting one's own good work particularly when one sees many people with bad intentions are successful.

One has to be alert on a 'conscious direction' and reinforce oneself in the path of goodness. Focus on being in the company of good is what the master is emphasizing on.

The good natured people's context for transformation is always alive and high. Our lives are run by our context. So often we find our context becomes a dead context and thus lose power to impact our lives meaningfully.

'Always the form of the Lord has to be meditated upon.'

In other words *Lord Vishnu* stands for the 'all-pervading consciousness.' It is this state of *being* that we have to experience, the all-pervading consciousness. The self is not limited by the body, mind or intellect. The self's true content and true nature is consciousness and consciousness that is beyond the body and mind.

As the self is not the object of any perceptions and hence has no form and thus the self is formless. Whatever is formless is all-pervading. This is the ultimate truth one has to realise.

'Wealth is to be distributed to the needy.'

Currency is like a current, it has to flow. Wealth not used for right cause amounts to abuse of wealth. One need not be against earning wealth, but one has to rightly use wealth. There is a great joy in giving.

'He gives not the best who gives the most, but he gives the most who gives the best. If I cannot give bountiful yet I will give freely and what I lack in my hand I will supply with my heart,' is one of the famous sayings.

Let our hearts guide our actions to give to the right cause. The heart knows the language of giving, the mind is always calculative. One's life should be a wise blend of both head and heart. Most of us work on building our head wisely but work seldom on our heart that gives. Thus, charity is a way of building our hearts and developing the emotional fitness.

Reflect on this story.

'I have to do service and serve the poor. I should be a good person. I should help others,' was the wish list of a student.

The master replied, 'If you drop the 'I', — service, goodness and helping nature would flow and follow you.'

VERSE 28

Why does one indulge in sinful behaviour?

सुखतः क्रियते रामाभोगः
पश्चाध्दन्त शरीरे रोगः
यद्यपि लोके मरणं शरणं
तदपि न मुञ्चति पापाचरणम् ॥
(भज-गोविन्दं... भज-गोविन्दं) (२८)

Sukhatah Kriyate Ramabhogah
Pascaddhanta Sarire Rogah
Yadyapi Loke Maranam Saranam
Tadapi Na Muncati Papacaranam
(Bhaja-Govindam Bhaja-Govindam...) (28)-

सुखतः – for the sake of happiness, क्रियते – (is done) one indulges in, रामाभोगः – sensous pleasures, पश्चात् – later on, हन्त – alas, शरीरे – in the body, रोगः – disease (comes), यद्यपि – even though, लोके – in the world, मरणं – death, शरणं – (is) the ultimate, तदपि – even then, न – (he) does not, मुञ्चति – leaves, पाप आचरणम् – sinful behaviour, भज – Seek, गोविन्दं – Govinda

One indulges in sensuous pleasures. Later on, alas, diseases take over the body. Even though in the world death is the ultimate end, even then an individual leaves not his wrong sinful behavior. (Seek Govinda, seek Govinda).

'Very readily one indulges in carnal pleasures. Later on, alas, diseases take over the body. Even though in the world the ultimate end is death, even then man leaves not his sinful behavior.'

Seek Govinda, seek Govinda.

Why does man indulge in carnal pleasures? Some seek power, some seek money and some seek fame. If we closely watch, in all the seeking what one truly seeks is internally a feeling of joy and inner fulfillment. Is it not?

The mind with its desire concludes joy is in pleasure, joy is in sexual intimacy, and joy is in this drug or power. The mind with its desire is the root cause of all problems because it tricks and directs one that the happiness is achieved only after the fulfillment of the desire. This is how the un-enlightened mind works. One has to see this clearly.

The mind loves someone and the same mind can hate the person at another point of time. So the mind has this polarity of love and hate in its swing. The mind that is seeking pleasure also has its opposite in it, where there is also pain. Every pleasure shows up like a coin which has the other side called pain.

Therefore, desiring for pleasure is inviting pain, as the other side of pleasure reflects pain, being two sides of the same coin. The mind has its opposites as polarities. So desiring for pleasure is inviting pain. Please see this very clearly. So living in the domain of the desiring mind is a life of deficiency — *samsara*.

Going beyond the mind is going beyond duality. Going beyond the mind is going beyond desiring. Going beyond the mind is going beyond one desiring for *this* or *that*.

If one does not desire how can one live in this world and survive?

There is another domain other than the domain of desire. That is the domain of the pure *'being.'* In that state one is only 'doing something' and 'wanting nothing.'

There can be action without desiring and its pollutions. Such action coming out of one's *being* is pure action not tainted by desire, but by inner intelligence. Such action is uplifting. An action out of desire is pressure and fulfilling desire only results in releasing that pressure created by desire.

One has to explore pure action coming out of one's *'being.'* Like there are so many bodily functions like one's breathing, functions of one's heart, the kidneys... that occurs without one desiring but as an expression of pure intelligence one is blessed with.

Similarly one's daily life's activities can happen in such a domain.

'Even though in the world the ultimate end is death, even then man leaves not his sinful behavior.'

The reason for such a paradox is due to one's addiction to sinful behavior. The moment one chooses to practice anything unconsciously it becomes his second nature.

For example, even in hot climate people smoke, it

becomes an addiction and then an addiction takes over oneself.

Everyone has a chief feature on which everything rests. One's chief weakness can be pleasure, sex, power and many more. One has to identify one's chief weakness which is the chief negative feature of oneself. One has to observe in one's daily life what those core features are.

Having identified them, the next step would be to observe and dis-identify from them. The art of disidentifying is called witness — *sakshi*. Without desiring, one has to see one's weakness by not adding any logic or references, but by just observing objectively. Slowly they would wither away and loose the grip on oneself.

Also one has to remember one's aim is enlightenment — *moksha*. Anchored in one's aim and dis-identifying the chief negative feature is one of the fundamental practices a spiritual person should engage in.

'Sinful behavior' is a foolish behavior. Let one see it as a foolish behavior, let it not be a mechanical behavior. Only then a magnetic center would open up in oneself and in such a space pure intelligence would flow or else foolishness would start parading in one's life.

Please understand that the pleasure of the body wears the body out. Learn to discover a joy that is beyond the body and the mind. Such an internal state is the state of *being* — *atmasithi*.

The central idea of vedantic teaching is true transformation, true change. The change is from worry to wisdom. Until such transformation happens one is nothing but an unfinished creation in this world. The real task is to complete oneself in discovering one's inner being as full and complete.

Until such change happen in one's actions, thoughts, and desires, one would go on searching for inner fulfillment.

And in such a search one develops a wrong habit which leads further to un-fulfillment, and thus an inner madness is built. Inner madness leads to sinful behaviour. Even if death were to come, the addiction to such foolishness makes one drunk and lost in the world of ignorance.

Just watch — whenever something goes wrong, there are indications of this phenomenon showing up. Worry is an indicator of sadness, frustration, feeling unfulfilled, internally stressed... Let these indicators help you to change.

Whenever you are on the right track, you will experience joy, gratitude, thankfulness and compassion. These are also indicators to be observed. Follow these indicators which will lead you to the path of light.

I heard a beautiful story.

A depressed man was drunk and had blisters on both sides of his cheeks. His friend asked him how it happened.

'My wife left a hot pan near the telephone. When the phone rang I accidentally picked up the hot pan,' replied the drunkard.

'What about the other cheek?'

'The blessed phone rang again,' replied the drunkard.

We need to drop our inner drunkenness in order to change our behaviour. The mantra is to change the state of *'being.'* The actions would then be transformed.

VERSE 29

Wealth and its mysterious ways of manifestation

अर्थमनर्थं भावय नित्यं
नास्ति ततः सुखलेशः सत्यम् ।
पुत्रादपि धनभाजां भीतिः
सर्वत्रेषा विहीता रीतिः ।।
(भज-गोविन्दं... भज-गोविन्दं) (२९)

Arthamanartham Bhavaya Nityam
Nasti Tatah Sukhalesah Satyam
Putradapi Dhanabhajam Bhitih
Sarvatraisa Vihita Ritih
(Bhaja-Govindam Bhaja-Govindam...) (29)

अर्थ — wealth, अनर्थं — (is) calamitous, भावय — (thus) meditate,
नित्यं — constantly, न अस्ति — there is not, ततः — from it,
सुखलेशः — (even) a little happiness, सत्यं — truth, पुत्रात्-अपि —
even from his own son, धनभाजां — to the wealthy, भीतिः — there
is fear, सर्वत्र — everywhere, एषा — this, विहीता — is (the ordained),
रीतिः — the way, भज — Seek, गोविन्दं — Govinda

*Wealth is calamitous (useless), thus meditate constantly; the truth is
that there is no happiness at all to be got from it. To the wealthy
there is fear even from one's own son. This is the way with wealth
everywhere. (Seek Govinda, seek Govinda).*

'Wealth is useless, thus reflect constantly: the truth is that there is no happiness at all to be got from wealth. To the rich, there is fear even from one's own son. This is the way of wealth everywhere.'

Seek Govinda, seek Govinda.

Even though it is said, 'Wealth is useless', what the master is trying to convey is that, what we are seeking is not sought through wealth. Wealth has its usefulness but what we are seeking is joy. When we seek joy through wealth we are missing the point. When we miss the point that we are seeking joy, seeking fullness, seeking wellness, then undue acquiring of wealth has a 'nuisance value.'

Understand this clearly. When you have abundant wealth you are stimulating jealousy in others, greed in others and other's greed and jealousy will thus be more of a 'nuisance value.' You will have to fear even your own son. A life filled with fear is not joy; a life filled with other's jealousy is not going to be comfortable.

Reflect on this tale as told by one of my students.

A student went to a master and pleaded the master to somehow cure his agonizing stomach ache. The master drew him closer. The master then picked up a big boulder and smashed it on his feet. The student screamed aloud in great pain.

'Why did you do that,' countered the student.

'Now you do not feel the stomach ache, but you have leg ache,' replied the master.

Sometimes, to get over one problem we get into another bigger problem.

To get over poverty one earns wealth and more wealth. It creates its own problems which is worse than having minimum wealth. Excess wealth is worse than scarce wealth.

To live a higher life, a classical life, a spiritual life, do not focus on accumulating excess wealth. Focus on simplicity. Make your life simple. Let your thinking be simple, have simple feelings. Drop the non-essentials and live with the essentials. The mind that hankers on the non-essentials is a complicated mind.

Such a complicated mind is an invitation to trouble and attracts unnecessary things in life.

Many people get hooked onto acquiring wealth, power, name, fame and this has more 'nuisance value' than true joy.

There is a collective unconsciousness about acquiring wealth and most of them are influenced by this unconsciousness. We are impacted by society, as what we discussed earlier as an 'environmental impact.' Society respects those who possess money, name, fame, power... and that pollution impacts one's mind. Be aware of such pollution is what the master is trying to unfold through this verse.

These are 'deadly habits' and not 'wise habits.' They ultimately take our lives. Be aware and life will be a great teacher.

Learn to 'listen to life.' Each moment it is expressing something useful. Do not be internally deaf so that you do not hear them.

Reflect on the story that I read in a cartoon book.

A guitarist was confident of his music. He boasted to a zoo keeper that if he plays his guitar even the lions would start dancing. The zoo keeper took his claim as a challenge. A live show was organised. A large crowd assembled to watch this phenomenon. A lion was sent.

Listening to the music the lion started dancing. The crowd was elated with joy and roar. Then the next lion was sent, who again started dancing the moment he heard the piece of music from the guitar. After some time another lion was sent. This lion straight away attacked the guitarist. Somehow with great difficulty the guitarist managed to save his life.

The zoo keeper confidently addressed the gathering, 'I was very sure, the lion sent last would attack him.'

'How did you know that?' asked many from the crowd.

'I made sure that the lion sent last was a deaf lion,' replied the zoo keeper with a cunning smile.

If one is deaf, one can never learn from life.

One has to observe one's inner drunkenness caused either by one's greed, or by ego or by jealousy. These create a false personality. Then an imaginary Self is created out of this false personality.

Such a Self creates an illusion and thus one goes on attracting such illusions. The false personality gives rise to wrong emotions and such emotions presents their own reactions. Thus one's false personality is based on pretence and one starts imagining that one knows something more than the others. This is how one's ignorance surfaces and resides in the core.

Observe, watch and dis-identify with this inner foolishness is what the master is trying to unfold.

VERSE 30

Practices for being centered and rooted

प्राणायामं प्रत्यहारं
नित्यानित्यविवेकविचरम् ।
जाप्यसमेत – समाधिविधानं
कुर्ववधानं महदवधानम् ।।
(भज-गोविन्दं... भज-गोविन्दं) (३०)

Pranayamam Pratyaharam
Nityanityavivekavicaram
Japyasameta Samadhividhanam
Kurvavadhanam Mahadavadhanam
(Bhaja-Govindam Bhaja-Govindam...) (30)

प्राणायामं – the control of all prana, प्रत्यहारं – the sense
withdrawal (from their respective sense-objects), नित्य अनित्य
विवेकविचरम् – the enquiry (reflection) consisting of
discrimination between the permanent and the
impermanent, जाप्य समेत समाधि विधानम् – along with japa and the
practice of reaching the total inner silence, समाधि, कुरु –
perform, अवधानं – with care, महत् अवधानम् – with great care, भज
– Seek, गोविन्दं – Govinda.

The practice of pranayama (control of prana), the sense withdrawal,
the enquiry into the permanent and impermanent, along with japa
and the practice of discovering inner silence — these perform with care
... with great care. (Seek Govinda, seek Govinda).

'The control of all activities, the sense withdrawal, the reflection, along with japa and practice of reaching *Samadhi* — inner silence, perform these with care... with great care.'

Now Adi Shakaracharya cautions, out of love and care that these practices should not be done mechanically but with awareness and understanding.

Any practice with understanding leads one rightly, or else the soul of the practice is lost. Thus one gets stuck to practise alone. This is how traditions are created. When the soul of the practice is lost, a tradition is born. Such traditions are nothing but blind traditions.

Reflect on the story that I read sometime back.

A master was giving a discourse in his monastery. During the time of discourse, a cat used to move around disturbing the proceedings. The master, out of concern for his students about their concentration being lost, told one of his senior students to tie the cat to a nearby pillar. Soon this became a daily practice during the discourse.

The master died a few years later. One of the students took over as the role of a teacher. Even then the same cat was tied to the pillar during the discourse. After some days the cat died. The student-turned-teacher ordered his fellow students to fetch a cat and tie him to a nearby pillar as this was their tradition and citing that his master used to do so during his discourses.

If one does not understand the soul of one's practices, the

misunderstanding as seen in the above example will occur again and again.

For example, pranayama is a practice of breathing, which is useful for overall health of the body and mind. The great saint Ramana Maharshi said, 'When one practices pranayama rightly, one's mind is caught like how a bird is caught in the net.' The thoughts per minute would come down in oneself through right practice. One of the major problems in modern day living is that one has too many thoughts and too many unnecessary thoughts.

There are too many unnecessary thoughts in one's mind. Most of our thoughts are a representation of an experience. Thus, the memory of a previous experience is silently hidden in a thought. So if one is not alert the past memory would influence the present experience. This clouds one's perception. The perception then will become foggy and distorted. This is the danger of many unnecessary thoughts.

As a principle, have a discipline to use thoughts only when required and when not required remain thoughtless. Pranayama — breathing practice helps us in this direction.

Pranayama generally includes four stages such as breathing in, breathing out, holding one's breath after breathing in — *antha kumbaka*, and holding one's breath after breathing out — *bahya kumbahaka*. The holding of the breath — *kumbhaka* is the danger part. When not done properly it can be harmful and to those with certain ailments like blood pressure, or a heart ailment, it can be very harmful.

There is another pranayama called *kapalabhati*, which is

rapid forceful exhalation. When not done properly it can be harmful, whereas when done properly it is extremely beneficial. Adi Shankaracharya says, be very careful. There are many practices which have to be done carefully with a correct understanding.

Thus, the caution is to be careful.

There are practices like sense withdrawal from the world of objects — *pratyahara*. This needs to be done wisely. Many people are addicted to be amongst crowds and not being amongst crowds, they feel lonely. One's identity gets defined by what people say about them as they are always surrounded by people.

Their identity is not a part of their clarity of understanding. It is essential to practice being alone at some point of time in a day. By this practice see yourself without much influence of people, of the maddening external crowd.

Not wisely practising this, the side effect of people being alone can lead to a habit of being indifferent to people. Being indifferent or being addicted is not wise living. A wise balance is required. Thus, any spiritual practice has to be done carefully. This is like a warning or advice from the great masters.

For example, repeating the name of the Lord — doing *japa,* is a beautiful practice. But there are people who go on repeating the name of the Lord so mechanically that they become inhumane to fellow beings.

A Russian poet narrated a beautiful incident. His mother used to watch the opera shows. There was an attendant appointed only to provide her tissue papers so as to wipe her tears while watching the show. She was feeling so oriented.

When she would get into her car to go back home during winter, there was another person waiting at the door of the car. His job was only to open the car door; even when snowing he had to wait at the parking lot near her car.

One day, the attendant out of sheer exhaustion could not bear the heavy winter and fell down while waiting. After the show, the lady came out and got into her car without even bothering to have a second look at her attendant who had fallen down.

'What type of feelings do you have Oh, Mother?' questioned the Russian poet.

In our tradition it is said, 'Serving humanity is serving God — *Nara Seva is Naryana Seva.*'

Engaging in *japa*, repetition of God's name and not being humane to other fellow beings is not true growth. We find plenty of such people around. In any practice one has to observe oneself very clearly.

VERSE 31

Master or a Teacher — who will lead you to Love for the truth... a Divine state

गुरुचरणांबुजनिर्भरभक्तः
संसारादचिराभ्दव मुक्तः ।
सेन्द्रियमानसनियमादेवं
द्रक्ष्यसि निजहृदयस्थं देवम् ।।
(भज-गोविन्दं... भज-गोविन्दं) (३१)

Gurucharanambujanirbharabhaktah
Samsaradaciradbhava Muktah
Sendriyamanasaniyamadevam
Draksyasi Nijahrdaystham Devam
(Bhaja-Govindam Bhaja-Govindam...) (31)

गुरु चरण अंबुज निर्भर भक्तः – great devotee of the lotus feet of the teacher, संसारात् – from the deficiency, अचिरात् – soon, भव मुक्तः – become free, सेन्द्रिय मानस नियमात् – through the discipline of the sense-organs and the mind, एवं – in this manner, द्रक्ष्यसि – you will experience, निजहृदयस्थं – that dwells in one's own heart, देवम् – the Lord, भज – Seek, गोविन्दं – Govinda

Oh, devotee of the lotus feet of the teacher! May you become free soon from the world of deficiency – Samsara, through the discipline of the sense organs and the mind. You will come to experience (see) the Lord that dwells in your heart. (Seek Govinda, seek Govinda).

'Oh devotee, in the lotus feet of the master may you become liberated soon from the life of deficiency – *samsara,* through the discipline of the sense-organs and the mind. You will come to experience the Lord that dwells in your own heart.'

Seek Govinda, seek Govinda.

The last four concluding verses are attributed to Adi Shankaracharya.

One has to understand the distinction between a master and a teacher. A teacher is interested in giving information while a master is one who works on one's transformation. A teacher is one whose knowledge dwells only in the intellect whereas a master is one whose knowledge descends from the *'intellect'* to *'feeling'* to *'being.'* A teacher is more interested in a tradition but a master is more concerned about the truth irrespective of what tradition one belongs to.

In the *Mahabharata* episode, Lord Krishna's communication with Arjuna is more from *being to being than intellect to intellect.* One can acquire more information and still be ignorant. The master is not focused on information but on one's state of *'being'*, so that existential ignorance can be destroyed.

Traditionally, it is said that a student has to become feminine so as to receive the knowledge from the master. One has to become the receiver. The master is a representation of pure emptiness as he is devoid of ego.

And at the same time he is full with the fullness of the

macro as there is no micro in him. A master's device is like a window leading one to the sky. By surrendering to the master one is led to God.

The Hassidic saying goes, 'When God gives something, He does not give to you, but through you.'

The role of a master is to awaken and in that awakening one becomes an absence but filled with Divine presence. This is a Divine art to be absent and at the same time be present. This is one of the greatest paradoxes of spirituality.

A true master disturbs one's inner sleep and makes one see dreams as dreams, false as false whereas a teacher leads one to dream and philosophises one's sleep. Therefore, see the distinction between a master and a teacher.

A true master pushes you to your inner depth and does not make you cling to him or dependant on him. Thus Adi Shankaracharya says, 'You will come to experience the Lord that dwells in your own heart.'

A student would always like to cling or hold onto a master. A teacher unconsciously or consciously exploits this inner state of a student.

In Buddhism, there is an expression that after the entire teaching it is said to the students, 'If you come across a Buddha, kill him.' The teachings, meanings do not depend on the external Buddha.

It is easy to worship someone but the master wants you to be in a 'state of a Buddhahood' and not just in the form of a Buddha. Hence, the emphasis is that all clinging

. should drop in the lives of the students.

The path is one of renunciation — s*anyas*, not in changing the outer or the dress but discovering true inner freedom in one's own being.

To discover this, one has to have inner fitness. Only then one's inner apparatus will be able to receive this Divine wisdom. It is like a computer having a modem to connect to the internet. This inner preparatory is the 'discipline of the sense-organs and the mind.'

The sense organs when not disciplined will bring unnecessary impressions from the outer world and fill the mind with garbage. This inner garbage will then stimulate one's mind into more thoughts.

Such a mind is a scattered mind. But an abiding and not a scattered mind is the spiritual necessity. The mind to abide in *here* and *now* requires stoppage of the scattered mind filled with external stimulants.

The saints in ancient India used to meditate in caves. The reason being to ensure all external stimulants through one's eyes, ears, smell ... would be minimized. One can discipline one's mind to be abiding in *here* and *now*. Such an abiding mind is a pure mind in which one can see the Divine in one's heart.

All these verses of this great text came from the experience of Adi Shankaracharya. He knew that inner freedom — *moksha* is not far away but right here in one's heart. It is like a seed that may feel the flower is very far from it but the flower knows that it is hidden in the seed.

The student may feel inner freedom is distant, enlightenment is a rarity, and a true master is hard to find. It is almost like how the seed feels the flower is far from it. But the reality is — flower is in the seed.

Similarly, freedom and enlightenment are not far away but it is right in one's heart. Adi Shankaracharya is like a flower and the students are like the seeds. The flower knows, the master knows and thus the expression 'you will come to experience the Lord that dwells in your heart.'

Develop love for such experience. Be sensitive to such a state of *'being.'* When one leads a sensible life, one develops healthy tastes. Love for the truth is a Divine taste. Do all your acts out of love and devotion. You will then have the right apparatus to see and experience the truth.

You will see without the seer, you will experience without the experiencer — the ego. Then there will be a pure seeing, pure experience. One will go beyond the seer, the experiencer — ego. One will experience such a wonderful truth that makes one revel in wonder.

Let these verses and their understanding bathe us and freshen our lives moment to moment.

A section of large crowd during Gita Talks by Swamiji

Two views of Prasanna Centre for Life Management

51, Ground Floor, 16th Cross,
Between 6th & 8th Main
Malleswaram, Bangalore 560 055, India

Tel: +91 80 4153 5832-35
Fax: +91 80 2344 4112
E-mail: prasannatrust@vsnl.com
www.swamisukhabodhananda.org
www.prasannatrust.org
www.ohmindrelaxplease.org

Prasanna Trust is a registered social charitable trust set up with the objective to re-look at various facets of Indian philosophy and culture for effective transformation of individuals in particular and the society in general.

We have made our presence primarily through :

• Transformative Education

• Social Oriented Service

TRANSFORMATIVE EDUCATION

a) MANAGING LIFE CREATIVELY

It is a 2-day workshop on personal effectiveness through interactions and meditations. An experience oriented, non-religious program designed to enhance productivity, handling stress, personal well-being and organisational synergy. It focuses on bringing forth the outer winner leading to creativity and an inner winner to meditative consciousness.

b) EXISTENTIAL LABORATORY

It is a 4-day residential retreat set amidst natural surroundings to experience oneself through a series of dynamic and passive meditations in order to see connectivity with nature, to heal and release the inner child, to realise innocence and wonderment in all walks of life based on the Upanishad truths — Chakshumathi Vidya.

c) CORPORATE HARMONY AND CREATIVITY

It is a 2-day comprehensive workshop for senior level executives to harness creativity and harmony in today's competitive work environment and preparing them for globalisation.

d) OH, MIND RELAX PLEASE!

It is a 1-day seminar based on unique techniques to transform from ordinary to extraordinary, dealing with fear and conflicts and converting them as challenges.

e) RELATIONSHIP MATRIX SEMINAR

An exclusive workshop to discover alchemy of different spectrum of relationship; be it father, mother, spouse, children, siblings, boss, subordinate colleagues, associate peers... so as to discover togetherness in a relationship.

f) MANTRA YOGA PROGRAM

A workshop based on five powerful Mantras to help in enhancing health, unlocking the blissful centre, increasing intuitive ability, creating wealth and divinity in oneself and others. This program is conducted in English and also in many Indian languages by well equipped students.

g) ART OF WISE PARENTING — The program will focus on importance of parenting, motivation, people skills, parenting as a learning journey, to operate from openness. Family Game as ice breakers — mainly to know each other. Empowering Parents to be skilled in employing various avenues for effectiveness. The program also focuses how to work on linguistic, spatial, musical, body, logical, perceptive and emotional intelligence of the child and also how to develop the capacity to observe the profound quality in a child like patience, passion, adventurous, exploring, systematic, expressive etc.

h) YOUTH PROGRAM

It is a 3-day program based on multiple intelligences. The program develops the hidden talent and skill in a child; to enable the child to face the world with confidence as each child is unique.

i) VISION 2020 - Youth Workshop for Empowerment

A three hour facilitation for brilliant young minds who are the torchbearers of Indian future growth with necessary skills to transform dream of "India being a superpower" into a reality.

Teachers, Parents, Administrators of educational institutions to please take note and support in spreading this message amongst the youth 15 years and above which constitutes vast majority of Indian population.

j) PRINCIPLES OF HEALING & GROWTH MANAGEMENT

The anatomy of an experience is explored in this workshop. The theory of chaos is transcended into an experience of cosmos. The principles of inner growth, drawing models from Indian heritage especially Vedas, and allowing one to have a 'peak experience' in and through the ups and downs of life is a unique driving skill. This creative living and enhancing growth is the 'context of all contexts' in which enlightenment is achieved in the already enlightened space. The teachings would be the both structured and flexible.

k) PRASANNA CENTRE FOR LIFE MANAGEMENT

* Unfolding the traditional texts of the Bhagavad Gita & the Upanishads as is relevant in today's living context.

* Workshops to bring forth creativity and awareness among youth, women and parents through a spiritual paradigm.

* Research to foster universal love through an inter-religious forum.

* Orientation programs for motivating social workers.

* Spiritual inputs to deal with phobia, fear, trauma, drug and alcoholic abuse.

* Research on aspect of applied Yoga and Meditation to foster healing process.

* Management programs for executives from Vedic perspective.

* The Vedic Centre of Management in essence, explores Vedic insights to manage oneself, family, work and metaphysical dimensions.

* Applying holistic vision of Indian heritage in all walks of life.

* Applying the Eastern wisdom for Spiritual counseling, Marriage counseling, Wise parenting and overall preparation of life.

* Fun oriented effective learning models of Eastern Management and programs for empowering teachers.

* Empowering young minds to be creative and effective in life.

SOCIAL ORIENTED SERVICE

a) CHILD CARE CENTRE – A HOME FOR HOMELESS – PRASANNA JYOTHI:

Nurturing lives of little angels who have been orphaned due to the paradox of circumstances. Uncared girls who otherwise would have withered away are growing into enthusiastic, intelligent, celebrative and responsible children.

b) VOCATIONAL CAMP FOR CHILDREN

In order to keep abreast with the fast changing face of

the world, it is proposed to equip the children of Prasanna Jyothi, various skills in office automation & allied area of skills. We seek support of individuals, business houses, institutions and invite them to be part of this noble vision of creating an atmosphere to impart our culture and thus contributing to the society we build.

c) PROVIDING ARTIFICIAL LIMBS AND CALIPERS:

Periodic camps are organized wherein people from impoverished background are given artificial limbs and calipers that help them to be dependent free. Some of the recipients have taken to work to earn their livelihood with the help of these support systems.

d) POOR FEEDING: Poor feeding camps are organized in different parts of various cities on a regular basis. Thousands are the beneficiaries of this.

e) SCHOLARSHIP: Under this scheme, meritorious students irrespective of caste, creed and religion but belonging to economically weaker section are provided with educational scholarships to enable them to a good career. This activity has benefited hundreds of students over the years.

Contribution to **Prasanna Trust** account is exempted from **Income Tax under Section 80 (G)**.

TITLES OF SWAMIJI'S WORKS
BOOKS

Oh, Mind Relax Please!
(also in Tamil, Telugu, Kannada, Malayalam, Hindi, Marathi, Gujarati & Bengali)

Oh, Mind Relax Please! — Part 2 *(only in Tamil, Kannada & Telugu)*

Oh, Life Relax Please!
(also in Hindi, Tamil, Telugu, Kannada, Gujarati and Marathi)

Meditation *(from Bhagavad Gita) (also in Kannada, Tamil, Telugu & Hindi)*

Stress Management- A bullet proof Yogic Approach (also in Kannada & Hindi)

Art of Wise Parenting *(also in Kannada & Hindi)*

Looking at Life Differently *(also in Tamil, Telugu, Kannada, Hindi & Marathi)*

Wordless Wisdom *(also in Tamil, Kannada, Hindi, Telugu, Marathi & Malayalam)*

Golden Words for Good Living

Karma Yoga *(based on Bhagavad Gita) (also in Kannada & Hindi)*

Roar Your Way to Excellence *(also in Kannada, Marathi, Hindi, Tamil & Telugu)*

Celebrating Success & Failure *(also in Kannada, Hindi, Marathi & Tamil)*

Harmonising Inner Strength *(also in Kannada, Marathi, Hindi & Tamil)*

Personal Excellence through Bhagavad Gita *(also in Kannada, Tamil & Hindi)*

Inspiring Thoughts for Harmonious Living

Agame Relax Please! *(in Tamil)*

Kutumbave Relax Please! *(in Kannada & Telugu)*

Elaignane Relax Please! *(in Tamil)*

Shiva Sutras - Divine Techniques for Enhancing Effectiveness (also in Kannada & Hindi)

Enhancing Life — The Art of Inner Awakening (also in Kannada, Marathi, Tamil & Hindi)

Clarity — An Inner Aliveness & Poetic Rambles from Life.

AUDIO
TRADITIONAL UNFOLDMENT

Gayatri Mantra *(also in regional languages)*

Maha Mruthyunjaya Mantra *(also in regional languages)*

Om Gam Ganapateya Namaha *(also in regional languages)*

Om Krishnaya Namaha *(also in regional languages)*

Om Shivaya Namaha *(also in regional languages)*

Healing Hurt through Gayatri Mantra

Handling Insecurity through Mruthyunjaya Mantra

Handling Crisis through Taraka Mantra

Mantra Yoga (Gayatri Mantra)

Mantra Yoga (Mruthyunjaya Mantra)

MEDITATION

Mahavisarjana Kriya

Navratri Upasana

Bhakti Yoga

Mantra Healing

Trataka Yogic Technique

Brahma Yagna

Meditation – the Music of Silence

Vedic Vision to Pregnant Women

Yogalaya

Seven Chakras of Hindu Psychology

A NEW LOOK THROUGH SPIRITUAL PARADIGM

Self Confidence through Hypnosis

Essence of Hinduism

Symbolism of Hindu Rituals

How to Deal with Fear

Stress Management

OCCULT TEACHINGS

LIFE Program

Guru Purnima

Mantra Chants

Who am I?

Shiva Sutras

Gita Talks

BHAJANS

Bhajans with the Master (Vol. 1)

VIDEO (in VCD form)

Get Rid of Stress – Stress Management through Spirituality

Jokes to Joy – Navarasas

Suffering to Surrender

Discouragement to Encouragement

Worry to Wisdom

Seeds of Wisdom

Looking Life Differently – Bhagavad Gita Chapter V

A Balanced Man

Inner Awakening

Harmony in Chaos

Shiva Sutras (Vol. 1 to 8)

Personal Excellence through Bhagavad Gita series

Living Consciously – Handling Inner Conflict (Vol 1 & 2)

Changing the Invisible Self (Vol 3 & 4)

Happy, Here & Now (Vol 5 & 6)

Being Open & Centered (Vol 7 & 8)

Ego – Edging God out (Vol 9 & 10)

Surging Joy - Within (Vol 11 & 12)

Joy in Detachment & Wonderment (Vol 13 & 14)

Three Realities (Vol 15 & 16)

Live Life Totally (Vol 17 & 18)

Integration of Roles – Great Transformation (Vol 19 & 20)

The Presence of the Present (Vol 21 & 22)

Attitudes towards Action (Vol 23 & 24)

Detachment in Actions (Vol 25 & 26)

Experiencing the Experience (Vol 27 & 28)

Unessential to Essential (Vol 29 & 30)

Witnessing Consciousness (Vol 31 & 32)

Inner Alchemy (Vol 33 & 34)

Transforming Mechanical Centres to Magnetic Centres (Vol 35 & 36)

Inner Strength... Silence (Vol 37 & 38)

Evolving Consciousness - Beyond Breakthroughs & Breakdowns (Vol 39 & 40)

Power of Will - Looking in Totality (Vol 41 & 42)

Ultimate Devotion - Pervasive Consciousness (Vol 43 & 44)

Swamiji's workshop empowers one to be Effective, Creative & Celebrative in all walks of life.

> **'LIFE' – a two-days workshop on how to use the mind for Success and Satisfaction**

Objective of the Seminar:
Outer Winner

- The art of powerful goal setting.
- Decision-making, Team building.
- Divine principles of worldly achievement.
- Interpersonal skills & Effective communication
- How to deal with difficult people.
- Possibility thinker.

Inner Winner

- The art of being blissful, restful and loving.
- The art of healing psychological wounds.
- Mind management.
- Worry management.
- Fear management.
- Meditation to bring about healthy inner healing and enlightenment.

What others say about the programme:

"Here's one Guru who's in tune with modern times."
— India Today.

"The unusual Swami from Bangalore is the latest Guru on the Indian Management scene."
— Business India.

"He has come to be hailed as the 'Corporate Guru'. The Management Swami has attempted to infuse the Corporate World with the much needed dose of ethics and spirituality."
— The Hindu.

Existential Laboratory
a four-day residential workshop

Amidst a carnival of natural surroundings, a series of passive and dynamic meditation facilitates one to:

- Replenish frozen tears with Warmth and Love.

- Hurts with Healing Touch.

- Rigidity with Flowingness & Childlike Innocence.

- Receiving with Giving.

- Seriousness with Playfulness.

- Knowledge with Wonderment.

- Confinement with Celebration.

- Withholding, with Let Go... in order to nurture one's 'being' centred in Restfulness.

For more details on Swamiji's in-house & public workshops contact:

PRASANNA TRUST
51, Ground Floor, 16th Cross,
Between 6th & 8th Main
Malleswaram, Bangalore 560 055, India
Tel: +91 80 4153 5832-35, Fax: +91 80 2344 4112
E-mail – prasannatrust@vsnl.com
prmadhav@vsnl.com
Visit us at www.swamisukhabodhananda.org
www.prasannatrust.org • www.ohmindrelaxplease.org

PRASANNA CENTRE FOR LIFE MANAGEMENT

#1, Nirguna Mandir Layout, Near I Block Park,
Koramangala, Bangalore – 560 047, INDIA
Phone: (080) 2552 6102

Please send me information on
☐ Seminar on LIFE program
☐ Workshop on E-Lab Program
☐ Seminar on Oh, Mind Relax Please!
☐ Seminar on Corporate Harmony & Creativity at work
☐ Books, Audio Cassettes, CD's, VCD's
Name:......................................
Title......................................
Company................................
Address..................................
....
City......................................
State .... Pin ....
Telephone...............................
Fax.......................................
Email.....................................

I know a few people who want to be benefited from Swamiji's program. Their names & Contact numbers are:

Name:.....................................
Tel:.......................................
Mobile:...................................
City:......................................
E-mail:....................................

Name:.....................................
Tel:.......................................
Mobile:...................................
City:......................................
E-mail:....................................

Name:.....................................
Tel:.......................................
Mobile:...................................
City:......................................
E-mail:....................................